THE POWER OF
PLACE

THE POWER OF
PLACE

Authentic Learning Through Place-Based Education

Tom **Vander Ark**

Emily **Liebtag**

Nate **McClennen**

 Alexandria, Virginia USA

1703 N. Beauregard St. • Alexandria, VA 22311-1714 USA
Phone: 800-933-2723 or 703-578-9600 • Fax: 703-575-5400
Website: www.ascd.org • E-mail: member@ascd.org
Author guidelines: www.ascd.org/write

Ranjit Sidhu, *Executive Director and CEO*, Stefani Roth, *Publisher;* Genny Ostertag, *Director, Content Acquisitions;* Allison Scott, *Acquisitions Editor;* Julie Houtz, *Director, Book Editing & Production;* Jamie Greene, *Associate Editor;* Judi Connelly, *Senior Art Director;* Khanh Pham, *Graphic Designer*; Kelly Marshall, *Interim Manager, Production Services;* Isel Pizarro, *Senior Production Specialist;* Trinay Blake, *E-Publishing Specialist*

All web links in this book are correct as of the publication date below but may have become inactive or otherwise modified since that time. If you notice a deactivated or changed link, please e-mail books@ascd.org with the words "Link Update" in the subject line. In your message, please specify the web link, the book title, and the page number on which the link appears.

PAPERBACK ISBN: 978-1-4166-2875-0   ASCD product #120017   n3/20
PDF E-BOOK ISBN: 978-1-4166-2876-7; see Books in Print for other formats.
Quantity discounts are available: e-mail programteam@ascd.org or call 800-933-2723, ext. 5773, or 703-575-5773. For desk copies, go to www.ascd.org/deskcopy.

Library of Congress Cataloging-in-Publication Data

Names: Vander Ark, Tom, 1959- author. | Liebtag, Emily, author. | McClennen, Nate, author.
Title: The power of place : authentic learning through place-based education / Tom Vander Ark, Emily Liebtag, Nate McClennen.
Description: Alexandria, VA : ASCD, [2020] | "ASCD product #120017" | Includes bibliographical references and index. | Summary: "The book offers a comprehensive and compelling case for place-based education and making communities the locus of learning for students of all ages and backgrounds"—Provided by publisher.
Identifiers: LCCN 2019046603 (print) | LCCN 2019046604 (ebook) | ISBN 9781416628750 (paperback) | ISBN 9781416628767 (pdf)
Subjects: LCSH: Place-based education. | Community and school.
Classification: LCC LC239 .V36 2020 (print) | LCC LC239 (ebook) | DDC 370.115—dc23
LC record available at https://lccn.loc.gov/2019046603
LC ebook record available at https://lccn.loc.gov/2019046604

────────────────────────

27 26 25 24 23 22 21 20   1 2 3 4 5 6 7 8 9 10 11 12

Emily: Thanks to all of those who have supported us throughout the process of writing this book and to those educators and students who are the inspiration for this work. To all of you, may I help you deliver on your own dreams in the near or distant future.

Nate: I would like to thank my family—Rachel, Kai, and Taya—for exploring our place with me through many adventures; my parents, who taught me the value of hard work, kindness, and the power of education; and all of the staff at Teton Science Schools for their contributions to a better world and their deep belief in place-based education.

Tom: Thanks to my parents for introducing me to the world—for decades of moving me outside my psychological and physical comfort zone to places where I could learn and grow.

THE POWER OF PLACE

AUTHENTIC LEARNING THROUGH PLACE-BASED EDUCATION

Acknowledgments ix

Preface: The Future of Place in Learning xi

An Introduction to Place-Based Education 1

1. Why Place Matters 9

2. Community as Classroom 21

3. Learner-Centered 38

4. Inquiry-Based 51

5. Local to Global 63

6. Design Thinking 74

7. Interdisciplinary 85

8. A Place-Based Education How-to Guide 98

Epilogue 131

Glossary 134

References 136

Index 144

About the Authors 153

Acknowledgments

We would like to acknowledge the countless educators who are providing young people with incredibly rich community-connected learning experiences every day. You fuel our work and provide us with hope, inspiration, and promise for a better future.

Thank you to all of the students who have inspired and challenged us along the way and to those who have made important contributions to their community and leaned into the power of place. We wrote this book for the millions of students who deserve better and richer learning experiences connected to their own communities.

We would also like to thank those who have supported our exploration, research, and writing. Thank you to ASCD for inviting us to write this book and to be a part of your exemplary cohort of authors. Thanks to the Getting Smart team, the Teton Science Schools team, the Carnegie Corporation, and others who started the push several years ago to amplify the place-based message, and who created many of the publications and resources mentioned in this book. Thanks to Carri Schneider for her contributions to the initial place-based campaign. We also want to acknowledge Education Reimagined for introducing us to students who are leading the way, many of whose stories and voices are featured in this book.

To the place-based pioneers who launched and have documented the modern educational system, including, among many others, Ray Barnhardt, Grace Lee Boggs, Greg Cajete, David Greenwood, Francisco Guajardo, Stephen Haymes, bell hooks, Oscar Kawagley, David Orr, Greg Smith, David Sobel, Paul Theobald, and Doris Williams—thank you for pursuing and prioritizing explorations of place. And thanks to the project-based learning pioneers who have inspired us.

We also recognize the thousands of community organizations, indigenous groups, informal and formal alliances, teachers, and schools that have implemented place-based education around the world for generations. This book is our humble effort to codify and advance the field to help more students learn locally.

And to our loved ones, we know we couldn't have completed this work without your understanding and support.

Preface: The Future of Place in Learning

Well, in the ancient world, the word *genius* was not so much used about individual people, it was used about places, and almost always with the word *loci*. Genius loci meant "the spirit of a place." And we all know what that intuitively means. We all have favorite places in the world, and it may be a seashore where you've got this ancient conversation between the ocean and the land and a particular geography of the way the cliffs or the beaches are formed. But it could've been the same in the ancient world. A little bridge crossing a stream with a pool at the back of it and a willow hanging over the pool; that place would be said to have a genius loci. But a more sophisticated understanding would [be that] it's this weather front of all of these qualities that meet in that place. So I think it's a very merciful thing to think of human beings in the same way—that is, your genius is just the way everything has met in you.

—**David Whyte,** *The Conversational Nature of Reality*

We have all experienced the power of place: those moments when we are fully alive; when the sights, sounds, and smells of an experience stopped us in our tracks; when learning was organic and visceral. It may be a strange new place where the culture and colors are unfamiliar and simultaneously delightful and disconcerting. Or it may be the mundane—an alley, a field, or a creek—seen with new eyes.

Place: it's where we're from; it's where we're going. Place comes in layers; it is old and new at the same time. Place is central to human development; it is how we comprehend the world; it asks for our attention and care. If we pay attention, place has much to teach us.

We have largely stopped making use of place in formal education. All the reasons were well-intentioned but industrial: abstracted frameworks, standardized measures, and efficient facilities. The addition of mobile technology, which has the power to unlock anytime, anywhere learning, is primarily used to provide useful differentiation, but the addition of screen time has (in most places) reduced, not increased, connection to place. Formal learning experiences that leverage the power of place are now the exception and not the rule. We hope to change that.

With this book and our related work, we seek to help educators, advocates, and parents connect children with places near and far. We hope for more engagement and authenticity in education. We seek expanded access to community-connected challenges. We aim to leverage local assets including parks, public spaces, museums, and businesses for learning.

Why Place Matters to the Authors

The power of place has been realized time and again by educators we work with. Place-based education also has been integral to our own learning journeys, careers, and lives.

Emily: In my first couple of years as an elementary school teacher, I didn't pay much attention to where students were from or their connection to their communities (although I should have). Once I realized the value and strengths of these connections, I had an entirely new perspective on teaching and learning. I began to realize the incredible amount of untapped potential and creativity in the students that I was trying to contain in my traditional, four-walled classroom. My own most powerful learning experiences have been deeply rooted in place and connected to my community—so why wouldn't this also be true for my students?

There is nothing more incredible than witnessing one of nature's finest phenomena, more invigorating than being uncomfortable and curious in a new culture or context, and more humbling than helping tackle an issue in your own community.

• • • • •

Nate: Something unexpected happens when you explore a community for the first time. Your worldview shifts with each question, each interaction, and each inquiry. You understand the place more deeply, and yet the deeper you go, the more you realize you have to learn. This is the power of place—it's an infinite mystery that continually leads to awe and wonder.

Pragmatically, my most important learning has come from place—in the outdoors, jobs, conversations, and explorations—all teaching skills and knowledge that were just as important as what I learned in school. I see that I can make an impact. I see that I can always learn. And I see that my actions create ripple effects across ecosystems and nations. This is what our young people need to learn—that they matter and that it starts with understanding and appreciating their local place.

• • • • •

Tom: I remember the sound of running water, the smell of damp logs, and the thrill of finding a tadpole in Sligo Creek. I was 11 and had time to dawdle. Years of battlefield and museum tours in and around Washington, D.C., introduced me to design and the way it can shape our lives. I knew I'd be an architect or engineer.

Awestruck a year later, I stood on a glacier at 14,000 feet, bracing against a 50-mile-per-hour wind and feeling very small against the vast expanse of the Colorado Rockies. Glaciology studies—that was the field for me (at least until frostbite and a girlfriend changed my mind). My interest in engineering and rocks sent me to the Colorado School of Mines and got me a good first job.

I'm the sum of the places I've been and the experiences I've accumulated. It wasn't my parents preaching contribution that convinced me of the merits of service; it was the urban ministries they brought me to for a decade. It wasn't a picture of the Rockies that won my heart; it was the paradox of fear and wonder that came with being in a spectacular remote setting. It wasn't any of the classes I took in college that I remember; it was work in strange and wonderful places that shaped my path. Place is powerful, personal, and persuasive.

• • • • •

We invite you to explore—or continue—your own place-based journey with us as you read this book and to reexamine existing beliefs about what is possible.

An Introduction
to Place-Based Education

Powerful learning has always been active and connected to place. From birth, children begin to learn from and with their surroundings. In the preindustrial age, the community was the classroom; children learned from their families about water, food, shelter, and play. Youth learned trades through apprenticeships.

The impulse to expand access to education in the mid-19th century began the process of industrialization of learning. Knowledge was the asset possessed by teachers and delivered to students. Instead of learning in the community, education became a formal system delivered to age cohorts that, like industrial products, were processed in batches through a standardized system. The community became less relevant as the industrial model of education emerged.

Schools became the places where parents sent their kids to learn instead of being just one aspect of learning. Church clubs, sports teams, scouting organizations, workplaces, and countless other out-of-school experiences continued, but they were considered extracurricular activities and no longer viewed as "learning." The emergence of service learning, field trips, and community-school models recognized that places were ripe areas for study and learner experiences, but these remained fringe activities.

Industrialized education walked away from authentic and connected learning. Efforts to promote and measure proficiency in basic skills had the unintended consequence of sanitizing and standardizing education while separating it from much that produces deeper learning and priority outcomes.

The rise of connected mobile devices paralleled the standards movement of the last 25 years. It held the potential to unlock anytime, anywhere learning, extend interactions, and personalize pathways, but its creative potential was overwhelmed by efforts to boost grade-level proficiency in basic skills.

Despite decades of distractions, connections to place remained strong around the edges—in rural schools, in career education, in early childhood environments, and among teachers committed to project-based learning. Restoring place to its central role in learning is a timely effort, given global interest in broader outcomes, increasing policy flexibility, and more learning options with mobile technology. In Chapter 1, we argue that extended community-connected challenges are the best way to build what have become the most important skills and dispositions for learners now and in the future—namely, agency, collaboration, and an entrepreneurial mindset.

We are living in an age when new educational models are being developed. Incorporating a new appreciation for the learning sciences, high-engagement progressions are designed and include better ways to provoke and measure learning. Place-based education sits firmly in the center of next-generation learning models and is a key to learner-centered school transformation.

Place-Based Education

Place-based education (PBE) "immerses students in local heritage, cultures, landscapes, opportunities, and experiences, using these as a foundation for the study of language arts, mathematics, social studies, science, and other subjects across the curriculum," according to the Center for Place-Based Education at Antioch University (Boggs School, n.d. b). We define it simply as anytime, anywhere learning that leverages the power of place to personalize learning—complementing the definition used by Teton Science Schools in Jackson, Wyoming: "[integrating] learning with place to increase engagement, learning outcomes, and community involvement" (Teton Science Schools, n.d.). Place-based education as explained by author Laurie Lane-Zucker (2016) is "the pedagogy of community, the reintegration of the individual into her home ground, and the restoration of the essential links between a person and her place" (para. 8).

Connecting projects to community, delving into authentic problems, and encouraging public products develop an ethic of contribution. "Solutions to many of our ecological problems lie in an approach that celebrates, empowers, and nurtures the cultural, artistic, historical, and spiritual resources of each local community and region," argues Lane-Zucker, who advocates that "schools and other educational institutions can and should play a central role in this process" (2016, para. 6).

Learning that leverages the power of place comes in many forms. As a result of our collective time spent as educators, researchers, designers, and leaders, we believe that the core of rich place-based experiences are the six design principles created by Teton Science Schools and used by the Place Network, a national network of small rural schools (Teton Science Schools, n.d.). The principles, shown in Figure 0.1, emerged from the work done within the Annenberg Rural Challenge in the 1990s, as well as from a set of principles created by a joint Teton Science Schools/University of Wyoming partnership in the 2000s. Although not all place-based experiences include a full manifestation of each one, the principles are often present to some degree when experiences are high quality and lead to meaningful student outcomes. Educators interested in connecting learning and community will find them helpful in grounding the design and implementation of place-based education.

FIGURE 0.1. The Six Design Principles of Place-Based Education

Community as Classroom—Communities serve as learning ecosystems for schools where local and regional experts, experiences, and places are part of the expanded definition of classroom.

Learner-Centered—Learning is personally relevant to students and enables student agency.

Inquiry-Based—Learning is grounded in observing, asking relevant questions, making predictions, and collecting data to understand the economic, ecological, and sociopolitical world.

Local to Global—Local learning serves as a model for understanding global challenges, opportunities, and connections.

Design Thinking—Design thinking provides a systemic approach for students to make a meaningful impact in communities through the curriculum.

Interdisciplinary—The curriculum matches the real world, with the traditional subject area content, skills, and dispositions taught through an integrated, interdisciplinary, and frequently project-based, approach in which all learners are accountable and challenged.

How to Use This Book

This book provides educators in *any* school context with an opportunity to see how they might begin to offer, or enhance, place-based learning. We intentionally chose to highlight schools that span varied geographic regions, private and public systems, and urban and rural contexts. We share stories from students who are from diverse backgrounds, have had varied learning experiences, and have attended different types of schools. Observers not connected with place-based education occasionally express a narrow view of the effort, portraying it as something reserved for those who have financial means to send students on expensive trips or for students who have already mastered basic skills and can "afford" to take time to explore the outdoors. We aim to counter that view.

We include a few place-based experiences that require international or domestic travel, but we focus more on providing examples of learning that can occur anytime, anywhere and are less dependent on special funding or having easy access to a particular environment. We also know there are schools finding ways to offer incredible place-based experiences that require a financial contribution, and we believe they are also important to include. Several chapters include a discussion of how and where mixed-reality and mobile technology can provide or enhance immersive experiences.

We also acknowledge and do not want to understate the real challenges that communities face that may inhibit the exploration of place (Nadworny, 2019). Although the majority of the discussions in this book focus on the opportunities available and ways to navigate potential barriers (see more on barriers in Chapter 8), we know that some students might not feel their home is safe, their perspective or history is valued, or their community is a place they want to spend more time exploring. We believe that agency, equity, and community all are enhanced with a place-based approach and will eventually lead to healthier and safer communities. (See Figure 0.2 for definitions of these terms.)

This book is structured so you can start with any chapter or read through from the beginning. Chapter 1 explains why place-based learning is important, relevant, and becoming easier to incorporate into learning journeys. In Chapters 2 through 7, we explain the six design principles of place-based education, including examples of how they are used in schools. Chapter 8 is a stand-alone how-to guide. An online microsite, www.gettingsmart.com/placebasededucation, complements this book and hosts resources mentioned in each of the chapters. The microsite icon is used to denote when a resource mentioned is available online.

FIGURE 0.2. Agency, Equity, Community: Definitions of Terms Related to Outcomes

Agency: *Agency* is the capacity and propensity to take purposeful initiative. It is the opposite of helplessness. Young people with high levels of agency do not respond passively to their circumstances; they tend to seek meaning and act with purpose to achieve the conditions they desire in their own and others' lives (Ferguson, Phillips, Rowley, & Friedlander, 2015). It is developed through activities that are meaningful and relevant to learners, driven by their interests, and often self-initiated with appropriate guidance from teachers. To put it simply, student agency gives students voice and, often, choice in how they learn.

Equity: The National Equity Project (n.d., para. 1) provides a working definition of *educational equity*:

Educational equity means that each child receives what he or she needs to develop to his or her full academic and social potential. Working toward equity involves:

- Ensuring equally high outcomes for all participants in our educational system; removing the predictability of success or failures that currently correlates with any social or cultural factor.
- Interrupting inequitable practices, examining biases, and creating inclusive multicultural school environments for adults and children.
- Discovering and cultivating the unique gifts, talents, and interests that every human possesses.

Community: Paraphrasing the Merriam-Webster online dictionary (https://www.merriam-webster.com/dictionary/community), a *community* is a group of people living in the same place or having a particular characteristic in common. It is also a feeling of fellowship with others, as a result of sharing common attitudes, interests, and goals.

Each of the design principle chapters (2 through 7) follows the same format (see Figure 0.3). Each opens with a powerful student story about place-based education. We then address one of the six design principles, explain what we mean by the principle, and highlight case studies of schools that have implemented place-based learning. Near the end of these chapters, we present helpful tips on how to implement that particular design principle and share more examples that illustrate what it looks like in practice. We conclude these chapters with a brief mention of how the principle connects to cognitive research and learning sciences (see the next section for more on the learning sciences).

Although this book is intended to be a practical guide, we believe the research underpinning all the information presented is incredibly important to keep at the forefront.

FIGURE 0.3. **Format for Chapters 2–7**

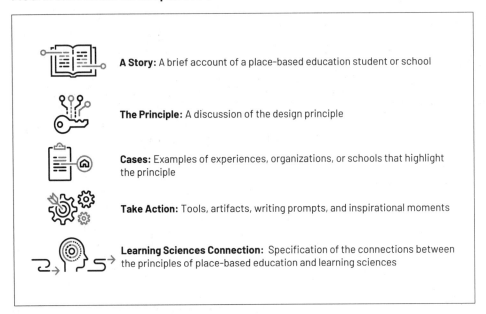

A Story: A brief account of a place-based education student or school

The Principle: A discussion of the design principle

Cases: Examples of experiences, organizations, or schools that highlight the principle

Take Action: Tools, artifacts, writing prompts, and inspirational moments

Learning Sciences Connection: Specification of the connections between the principles of place-based education and learning sciences

Learning Sciences

The learning sciences—the study of how humans learn—provide us with empirical evidence that place-based education has merit and helps students reach academic milestones. As noted earlier, we reference connections to the learning sciences throughout the chapters on the place-based education principles. More specifically, we cite *Designing for Learning*, a synthesis of learning science research by Jennifer Charlot, Cynthia Leck , and Bror Saxberg (2018). Figure 0.4 presents the learning science principles delineated in *Designing for Learning*, and Figure 0.5 shows how they align with the principles of place-based education.

FIGURE 0.4. **Learning Sciences Principles**

Cognition: Cognition refers to the set of processes by which learners take in new stimuli, process these stimuli into memories, and retrieve these memories to deploy in future actions.

- Principle 1: Focused Attention. People learn best when they direct their focus toward the content and experiences most relevant to learning.
- Principle 2: Manageable Cognitive Load. People learn best when they are challenged but are processing a manageable amount in their working memory.
- Principle 3: Meaningful Encoding. People learn best when new learning is experienced in memorable ways and is related to prior knowledge.
- Principle 4: Effective Practice. People learn best when they practice challenging-but-doable skills at frequent, focused intervals and across diverse contexts.
- Principle 5: High-Quality Feedback. People learn best when they receive timely and targeted feedback to guide their improvement.
- Principle 6: Metacognitive Thinking. People learn best when they are able to plan, observe, evaluate, and adjust their own learning processes.

Motivation: The willingness to start, put in mental effort, and persist, even in the face of challenges.

- Principle 7: Value. People learn best when they find the content, outcomes, processes, and relationships associated with learning to be important and valuable.
- Principle 8: Self-Efficacy. People learn best when they believe in their ability to grow and achieve mastery of what they are learning.
- Principle 9: Sense of Control. People learn best when they perceive that they have meaningful and appropriate agency over their learning.
- Principle 10: Constructive Emotions. People learn best when they are in constructive emotional states versus feeling excessive stress or anxiety.

Identity: Identity stems from how learners—and those around them—make meaning of their unique combinations of personality traits, physical characteristics, group memberships, values, beliefs, attitudes, and life experiences.

- Principle 11: Self-Understanding. People learn best when they have a deep understanding of who they are and can use this knowledge to maximize their learning.
- Principle 12: Sense of Belonging. Students learn best when they feel connected to, and accepted by, the people and environment around them.
- Principle 13: Navigating Identity Threats: People learn best when negative beliefs associated with their identity are minimized or buffered against.

Individual Variability: The various cognitive, social, emotional, and physical ways by which individuals differ that affect—and are affected by—the environments, experiences, and relationships they encounter throughout life.

- Principle 14: Life Experiences. People learn best when their unique life advantages and adversities are understood and responded to.
- Principle 15: Developmental State: People learn best when their experiences align with where they are developmentally.
- Principle 16: Learning Differences: People learn best when their unique learning needs are identified and resources and supports are aligned with these needs.

Source: From Designing for Learning (pp. 8–11), by J. Charlot, C. Leck, and B. Saxberg, 2018, Transcend. Copyright 2018 by Transcend, Inc.

FIGURE 0.5. **How Place-Based Design Principles Align with Learning Sciences Principles**

Place-Based Design Principle	Learning Sciences Principles			
	Cognition	Motivation	Identity	Individual Variability
Community as Classroom	3	7	12	14
Learner-centered	2	8, 9	11	14, 15, 16
Inquiry-based	3	7, 9	12	14
Local to Global	3, 4	7	12, 13	14
Design Thinking	4, 5	7, 9, 10	12	14
Interdisciplinary	2, 3, 4	7	12	14, 15, 16

1

Why Place Matters

"My experience with place-based education prepared me to thrive in every aspect of my being," said high school student Elizabeth Irvin (2018, para. 6), after CITYterm, an immersive project-based learning experience in New York City. It combines city expeditions with seminars and meetings with politicians, artists, urban planners, and authors.

Irvin said the six-day experience uncovered new academic interests that she may pursue as a career. She added, "Discovering my passion for alternative learning styles has played a large role in my college search" (2018, para. 6).

The experiences that shape our lives almost always include relationships—with someone who walked alongside us, someone who expanded our horizons, someone who inspired us. In addition to people, shaping experiences are often connected to places—a gallery, theater, workplace, soccer pitch, clearing in the woods, or mountain trail. Sometimes that shaping place is at school, but the thesis of this book is that the entire community is a classroom worth connecting with and that place is an integral component of youth development.

This chapter addresses three questions: What does place do uniquely well? Doesn't technology make place irrelevant? Why is place important now?

The following sections make the case that place is important, relevant, and timely. More specifically, place promotes agency, equity, and community;

it provides a compelling context for learning; and it is bolstered by current trends in practice, policy, and technology.

Place Promotes Agency, Equity, and Community

Context matters. Although time spent in the community or on a trip to another community seems academically "expensive," place is uniquely efficient at delivering value to young people and the places they engage with. Every community and place has a unique ethos, ecosystem, and combination of assets and challenges. Connecting young learners to their community and enabling them to immerse in other communities near and far promotes the foundational goals of public education: agency, equity, and community. Engaging young people in exploring place stands to benefit us all.

Agency

Marie Bjerede progressed from an engineer to a high-tech general manager because she had great technical skills and the ability to communicate and collaborate. Leading Qualcomm's Design Center, she studied human motivation and became an early advocate of self-organizing teams. Bjerede found that in attacking adaptive problems, it was creativity and collaboration that mattered. The most successful engineers didn't wait to be told what to do; they understood the goals and took initiative. It's this sense of *agency*—the ability to act on the world—that, according to Bjerede, will be the most important employment skill. It's a confidence that we can affect our future and our surroundings (Getting Smart Staff, 2018a, para. 3).

Agency requires self-knowledge, social awareness, and a sense of place and time. It is an applied disposition gathered through successively larger actions on a progressively larger world. What teaches us to perceive our location and relations is not language; it is our physical senses collecting action research. Agency is a muscle; place-based learning is the gym.

Many schools value routine and compliance—and both squelch student agency. It's extended encounters with novelty and complexity that build the disposition and skills of agency—the humility to appreciate the complex and the confidence to know what to do next. These valuable extended challenges are frequently connected to a community that provides context for learning and opportunities for contribution. Once students feel ownership in a space and feel valued, agency can begin to develop through these powerful learning experiences.

Equity

At the core of place-based education is the need for more equitable learning environments for all students—environments where students are seen, valued, and heard. In these environments, learning is designed with and for students as humans and individuals in the space. This is deep and complex work, but it should be at the core of why we choose to work with young people. Utilizing place is one way to do this.

Young people from affluent households often experience a rich variety of places both locally and internationally that are not easily accessible to those less fortunate. A school's systematic commitment to expose children to a variety of community assets closes a portion of this opportunity gap. An example is a commitment by the city of Tacoma, Washington, to allow every preschooler in the city to spend a week learning at the zoo.

People who grew up experiencing racism or intolerance may feel like something—and some place—has been taken from them. Beyond providing access, community learning experiences can create enfranchisement—the sense that "people like me" belong here, whether that's at the zoo, a museum, city hall, or a high-tech workplace.

Each learner is unique, and equity demands that we meet every child where he or she is—emotionally, cognitively, economically, and geographically. Connecting learners to the place where they live can contribute to a sense of identity—a sense of who they are and where they're from. The humblest settings and surroundings have something to teach. And learning about a new place may be the best way to illustrate and support the variability in the way humans perceive and process an experience.

We cannot assume that everyone has the same access to opportunities and networks (Fisher & Fisher, 2018). By engaging students in place, we increase their ability to have meaningful experiences and build social capital (see page 12 for more details). Work-based learning and community service are examples of experiences that extend social networks and may expand future opportunities.

Place-based experiences can directly confront factors that have been oppressive or limiting for communities. For example, Vaux High School is a partnership between the School District of Philadelphia, the housing authority, the teacher's union, and Big Picture Learning. Students engage in extensive internships and benefit from on-site partners that provide youth and family services (Vander Ark, 2018d). "We created a place kids want to be. We created ownerships through internships," said executive director David Bromley (Vander Ark, 2018d, para. 9).

Community

Place-based education connects learning to communities and the world around us; it builds community in four respects:

1. **It creates bonds.** When a group experiences the wonder of a vaulted ceiling, mountain vista, or night sky, it creates a special bond. Whether it's the challenge of navigating a subway or trailblazing in the woods together, these moments of shared struggle or awe can act as a glue that connects people and builds community. Early childhood education environments often use community as the basis for teaching and learning throughout the year, grounding each experience in how we can work together and create common norms and culture.

2. **It personalizes learning.** Place-based learning allows students to find a personal connection to their community or a place. With some voice and choice in shaping projects, internships, and service experiences, learning is personal and community connected.

3. **It builds social capital.** With intentionality, place-based learning helps young people develop their social networks and take the chance out of chance encounters beyond school.

   Julia Freeland-Fisher, director of education at the Clayton Christensen Institute, became interested in social capital after learning that more than half of all job placements result from a personal connection—and that schools just aren't set up to influence this critical success factor. She notes that schools may be social, but most are insular. Imagine the community that could be created if, through a series of internships, site visits, and community-connected projects, each high school graduate left school connected with 100 community leaders or professionals—locally and regionally.

4. **It promotes contribution.** Some schools treat students as participants preparing for a distant future. Place-based learning helps young people identify opportunities and make community contributions in the present—powered by new technologies that make it easier than ever to code an application, launch a campaign, or start a business. When empowered with a sense of agency and supported with time and tools, young people can contribute to their community in unprecedented ways.

With repeated place-based experiences, young people are cocreating the future. In a world that is becoming more individualistic, place-based learning invites young people into the community. Learning in a variety of places with a wide range of people builds agency, equity, and community.

Place Provides a Compelling Context for Learning

With a global economy and technology that connects almost everyone and extends learning and work opportunities, one could ask, "Isn't place less relevant?" In fact, community-connected learning is more relevant than ever because it offers a unique context for learning through four dimensions: motivational, instructional, environmental, and cultural (see Figure 1.1).

Place Is a Motivational Context

Think of your most memorable learning experience. It might have been in school—an experiment or a writing assignment—but chances are it was extracurricular or out of the ordinary. It was probably rooted in relationships and involved an authentic challenge. It may have been associated with a place.

Places have the ability to create a sense of awe and wonder—as might occur in a great hall for a musical performance, when viewing a mountain vista, or in the boundary spaces between sea and land. Places can also provoke anger and concern—for example, a polluted stream, the site of an obvious injustice, or a location marred by a dangerous condition—that, in turn, may promote study and action.

Moments of awe or anger, coupled with student-led inquiry, can fuel meaningful, deeper learning. Our inherited school structures tend to squeeze out place-based experiences (which are more common in the primary years) with a

FIGURE 1.1. **Context and Place-Based Learning**

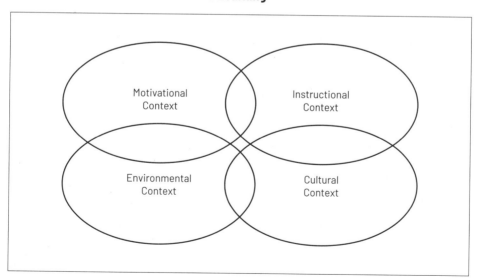

Place-based learning promotes agency, equity, and community by offering a compelling context with four dimensions.

focus on content transfer. The cumulative effect of well-intentioned efforts has led to less focus on the outcomes that matter most and the experiences most likely to deliver them.

Place Is an Instructional Context

For teachers at High Tech High in San Diego, California, place is the palette and the city is the text. Students in the High Tech High network (four campuses total) benefit from museum partnerships, watershed studies, community-connected impact projects, and business partnerships (Liebtag, 2019).

The 200 schools that belong to the nationwide New Tech Network (90 percent of which are district schools) share outcomes that matter, teaching that engages, culture that empowers, and technology that enables. New Tech students participate in project-based and place-based learning experiences that leverage partnerships and community assets to make learning authentic and meaningful (Vander Ark, 2017). Teachers in New Tech schools engage in place-based learning including site visits and walking tours (McBride, 2016).

Whittle School and Studios is a global school network. Initial host cities of Washington, D.C., and Shenzhen, China, comprise a platform for understanding how communities work, for integrating classroom learning with the life of the world, for addressing global challenges, and for cultivating the awareness to become socially responsible global citizens. Whittle campuses have a weekly Expeditionary Day when students engage with questions from their peers or of their own design, both by working outside the classroom within the larger school community and by engaging the people, places, politics, and peculiarities of their city. Students can study at other Whittle campuses, each with their own Center of Excellence, with a theme based on local strengths (Getting Smart Staff, 2018b).

The Place Network is a collaborative network of rural schools that connect learning and communities to increase student engagement, academic outcomes, and community impact. They share an integrated project-based approach to community-connected learning.

These four school networks and many others believe that project-based learning is an effective way to build student agency, persistence, and project management skills and to apply communication and problem-solving skills. Many projects are community connected and use place as an instructional context.

Place-based learning uses the city or town as the classroom. It leverages local assets and partners in learning and connects local issues to global themes. It situates extended integrated challenges in a local ecosystem.

Place Is an Environmental Context

We live on a complicated planet—one that humans are just beginning to understand but increasingly influence. The Fourth U.S. Climate Report indicates rapid (and predictably catastrophic) changes and a decline in the overall health of the environment. Recent years were the hottest on record, with more than the usual number of natural disasters, such as fires and tropical storms (Reidmiller et al., 2018, p. 37). It appears that young people will continue to experience more extreme weather and the unpredicted collisions of manmade and natural systems.

The combination of increasing natural and manmade shocks will damage regional economies—and perhaps the global economy. As a result, there is an increased need for more community connections, along with more agility and adaptability.

The State Education and Environment Roundtable (SEER) sponsors a network of schools around the Environment as an Integrating Context (EIC) model for improving student learning. Launched in 1995 with support from The Pew Charitable Trusts, more than 200 schools are involved in the network.

The interaction of humans, nature, and built communities is extraordinarily complex. It involves the economic, cultural, and ecological forces at work in a region. Young people deserve the owner's manual for the place they are inheriting. That means studying place from all three vantage points.

Place Is a Cultural Context

Culture forms the foundation for behavioral norms—the unspoken rules of conduct and shared social conventions. Because culture matters to human development at the macroeconomic level and to identity development at the individual level, it is worth studying. Given the complexity of culture, immersive experiences are far better than a textbook at provoking deep and integrated learning about culture.

Ladson-Billings (1995) reminds us that for centuries, groups of people have used their culture as the starting point for learning about and understanding the world and then incorporated education. She contends that all too often, educational systems try to insert culture into education when we ought to be using culture as the context and viewing education through place.

Travel-based learning—even the virtual variety—builds empathy and cultural competency. When combined with language acquisition, it produces global competence that helps young people become productive contributors on diverse teams (Liebtag, 2015). According to Deardorff (2009), these experiences grow competencies that include cultural understanding and knowledge, self-awareness, openness, respect for different cultural norms and practices, and positive feelings about interacting with people from different cultures. This deep reflection about our own culture, communities, and contexts adds to the power of place-based learning.

Navigating a new city and culture develops wayfinding abilities, skills, and dispositions that are critical for young people who will face waves of complex change. As identified by Next Generation Learning Challenges, "wayfinding abilities" include surveying the landscape, spotting opportunities, asking for help, and making good decisions (NGLC MyWays, n.d.). Studying a place and its culture may be the best way to develop these wayfinding skills.

These four contexts—motivational, instructional, environmental, and cultural—interact with one another to make each and every place a useful learning location.

Place Is Bolstered by Current Trends in Practice, Policy, and Technology

Engaging in places near and far is becoming easier and more important than ever. Trends in practice, policy, and technology are aiding place-based education. As shown in Figure 1.2, four key factors are driving the future of place-based education: (1) personalized learning, (2) competency education, (3) mixed

FIGURE 1.2. **Drivers That Bolster Place-Based Learning**

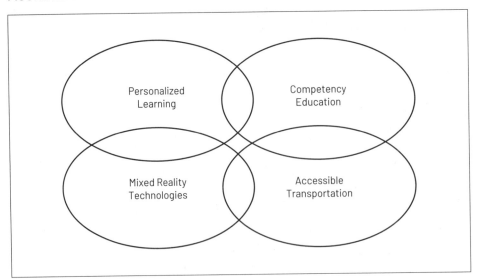

Place-based learning is bolstered by four drivers.

reality technologies—the merging of real and virtual worlds, and (4) accessible transportation.

Personalized Learning Benefits from Place

One of the most popular trends in American education today is *personalized learning*. In the narrowest sense, the term is used as a synonym for *blended learning*—a mix of adaptive technology and small-group instruction aimed at reading and math targets.

The skill-building sprints of personalized learning provide an on-ramp for full participation in project-based and place-based challenges. For example, before a planned water-quality analysis, some students need to catch up on data analysis techniques so they can fully contribute to their team's effort.

Advocating a broader view, iNACOL (the International Association for K–12 Online Learning) says, "The purpose of personalized learning is to open student pathways and encourage student voice and choice in their education" (Abel, 2016, para. 6). It defines personalized learning as "tailoring learning for each student's strengths, needs, and interests—including enabling student voice and choice in what, how, when, and where they learn—to provide flexibility and supports to ensure mastery of the highest standards possible" (Abel, 2016, para. 5).

In this broader view of personalized learning, "school" is no longer a physical space but an anytime, anywhere learning journey varying by path, pace, and place. Personalized learning not only sets up place-based education but also provides the full context for personalization.

In some cases, a teacher chooses a place for a class or team to study. In other cases, students have the option to choose a site or community partner. Even during whole-group work, each person experiences place in an individual way. It's this context that helps develop a student's fuller sense of identity, which leads to agency.

A growing number of schools are not just using whole-group activities but also returning to team projects (or are going back to project-based learning after years of focusing on only core math and literacy skills) because this approach provides application and integration of knowledge and skills. A high-quality project requires students to think critically about a complex problem, question, or issue with multiple answers and then to work on that project over the course of days, weeks, or even months. A project-based approach promotes persistence and collaboration and teaches project management skills.

A high-quality project also reflects what happens in the world outside school. It uses the tools, techniques, and technology found there and can both make an impact on other people and communities and connect to the interests and concerns of young people (High Quality Project Based Learning, n.d.).

Competency Education Unlocks the Potential of Place

For more than a century, schools have marked learning in time-based credits. As the world shifts to better measures of demonstrated capabilities, it has begun to unlock anytime, anywhere learning. With commonly recognized measures, learners can develop competencies in a wide variety of settings and accumulate those competencies in a secure, portable profile.

As competency systems mature, learners have more community-based learning opportunities. An early example is LRNG, a nonprofit (now part of Southern New Hampshire University) that extends learning experiences to urban youth. Students complete playlists of digital and physical experiences and earn badges that unlock employment opportunities and may be combined to earn college credit. Similarly, by means of community-connected challenges, students can earn competency credits in writing, math, and science as a result of their demonstrated learning.

Personalized and competency-based learning is also changing the place called school. Around the world, schools are moving away from long hallways lined with identical classrooms to more flexible learning spaces that facilitate project-based learning and competency-based progressions. Students move from project teams to skill groups to activity centers while building skills and developing agency and self-management.

Flexible seating is a big part of this trend. Not every school can afford to remodel or build new facilities, but many have added new seating options—including a mix of high- and low-top tables, hard and soft seating—that give students choice in how and where they work (Vander Ark, 2018f, para. 3).

Mixed Reality Extends Immersive Experiences

Place-based learning is immersive. The technology of mixed reality can extend and enhance those immersive experiences and will likely increase the power of place in the future.

On screen. Rich video can introduce a place or explain a place-based phenomenon. National Geographic, for example, has an extensive library of videos covering geology, geography, and ecology. Video is frequently used to add cultural relevance to language instruction.

Augmented screens and spaces. As half a billion people have experienced by playing *Pokémon Go*, augmented reality (AR) allows you to place holograms in the space around you to blend people, places, and objects from the physical and digital worlds. Google has more than 150 AR experiences that bring to life animals, human physiology, history, and natural phenomena (everything from mitosis to *Moby Dick* to modern art). It makes possible what once would have been impractical or dangerous—like viewing a swirling tornado or bringing a buzzing beehive into your classroom.

Using the Google Expeditions app, teachers and students can connect on the same network and take on the roles of "guide" and "explorer." Teacher guides can lead explorers by following the script and guiding questions, or they can use the accompanying audio narration (Poth, 2018, para. 4). The future of place-based education will likely blend these experiences with the physical presence in a place.

Immersive screen. Virtual reality (VR) allows users to step into immersive environments. It is particularly well suited to taking students into imagined worlds (e.g., science fiction), dangerous worlds (e.g., flight simulation, military actions), places that are difficult to visit (e.g., deep sea, mountain peaks), and gamified experiences. Immersive training has long been used in aviation and military training, where risks are high and where experiencing an unlikely failure may nevertheless be a valuable lesson. As costs of equipment and experience development have dropped, VR has become widely used in industrial training.

With a smartphone and a cardboard viewer, Google Expeditions offers more than 900 virtual reality field trips. Tours are related to famous locations, and students can learn about global initiatives and explore career pathways. Likewise, the Nearpod VR library includes lessons in social studies, science, and life skills, as well as college tours.

Anson Ho, program manager for Microsoft, is encouraged by early classroom applications of mixed reality, which suggest improved engagement and outcomes for students. He sees potential for more academic growth in classrooms and to transform distance learning.

Mixed Reality Enhances Place-Based Learning

Mixed reality technology can enhance, supplement, and extend place-based learning. Specifically, it

- Provides immersive cultural experiences in places a student has not visited.

- Introduces and explains new concepts in compelling 3D format.
- Empowers interaction and collaboration with others during an immersive experience.
- Enables co-solving challenges and working with schools in other places.
- May include gamified elements that boost engagement and persistence.
- Allows students to create videos and immersive experiences to share their perspective.
- Provides deeper experiences that can be easily repeated.

Accessible Transportation Will Extend Access

Transportation is one of the biggest challenges to making the community the classroom. However, as rideshare applications expand and begin to incorporate autonomous vehicles, transportation will become less expensive and more accessible. This expanded access to transportation will have a profound effect on secondary education. Many students will have better access to work-based and service-learning experiences, and community assets, including parks, museums, libraries, and cultural centers, will be more accessible. As competency systems expand, it will become easier not only to travel to an alternative learning site but also to demonstrate new skills, earn a badge or credit, and have that learning be widely recognized.

Summary

As educational models further embrace deep connections to place, entire ecosystems become classrooms, and agency, equity, and community are developed for all learners. The four contexts of place-based education—motivational, instructional, environmental, and cultural—are enhanced as this approach to education expands. The future of place-based education will be driven by trends in practice, policy, and technology in four realms: personalized learning, competency education, mixed reality technology, and accessible transportation.

2

Community as Classroom

Our ultimate end must be the creation of the beloved community.

—**Martin Luther King Jr.**

Marcus, a native Californian, realized his potential to contribute to the world as he sat alone by the Colorado River, reflecting on a group project he had worked on for six months. Alongside a team of four, including a national park ranger, Marcus served as an interpretive ranger answering questions for visitors and teaching classes in the junior ranger program for kids.

When he completed this place-based project, Marcus was a student at Eagle Rock School, which is a school in Estes Park, Colorado, that primarily works with youth who have not succeeded in traditional K–12 classroom settings. The national park experience is just one of many he had while at Eagle Rock. Marcus is currently thriving at Antioch College in Yellow Springs, Ohio.

Sharing his thoughts, Marcus said this:

When I think about place-based education, I think [about] being in the mountains at Eagle Rock and Rocky Mountain National Park. It took me to a different place and opened me to different things.

I learned how to work with others in a different environment. It was a nice way to use something that I already knew, but it became enhanced doing it in that context. I learned more and had fun doing it. I wanted to go to class; it didn't feel like a hassle. (personal communication, January 20, 2019)

The power of the learning experiences at Eagle Rock is not only that they are embedded in, and designed with, the community but also that each student becomes an integral member of the community during the time spent there. As a result, most students leave saying that they know themselves as leaders who are constantly learning in the real world.

Real projects in real communities like the one Marcus experienced increase engagement and agency for students. As a core principle of place-based education, Community as Classroom reminds us as teachers that all students want relevance and that all places can be classrooms.

 ## The Principle: Community as Classroom

As infants, humans have an insatiable curiosity about the world around them. Over time, the lens narrows based on experience, environment, and privilege. Some worlds expand and others shrink. Despite a changing and variable perspective for students, each place can be viewed from the three components of the Place Triangle—ecology, culture, and economy—that are found across cultures, geographies, and time (see Figure 2.1). These three components intersect to describe a place. Ecological elements consist of the natural world within a place. Cultural elements consist of the human-built factors (including political and social) that affect a place. Economic elements, although certainly human built, are enough of a driver to cite specifically when describing a place.

As learning embeds within a community, students consider each of the three components of the Place Triangle to understand the function of a place at a given moment in time. From that understanding, a student can begin to ask questions about past and future conditions: How has the economy changed over time? How has this change affected the local ecology, and vice versa? Given an understanding of the past and present, how might this place look in the future?

As the expanded view of the classroom develops, students and teachers can imagine increasingly complex and novel learning experiences. Starting with early childhood education, we often use place-based experiences that are aimed at

FIGURE 2.1. **The Place Triangle**

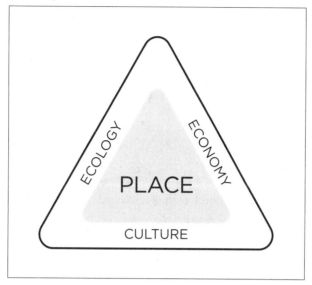

Source: Used with permission from Teton Science Schools, Jackson, WY.

expanding students' views of the world, engaging them in outdoor learning, and relating our learnings back to our community. Well-known and proven models such as Montessori and Reggio Emilia retain place at the core of their practices (Holland, 2019). Finland, Australia, and other countries have long used outdoor and place-based experiences to drive student engagement and richer learning experiences (Walker, 2016). In the United States, newer early childhood centers and programs such as Tinkergarten and "forest kindergartens" blend new models and technology with place (Tinkergarten, n.d.; Wikipedia, 2019).

Unfortunately, as learning progresses and students move on to primary and secondary education, we often begin to neglect the importance of place (Williams, 2018). However, we know place-based education can be done at all ages and at all levels of learning. For example, consider an ecology unit in a high school biology class filled with unfamiliar vocabulary and concepts such as energy flows, ecotones, and habitats—all packaged into an end-of-unit exam. Instead of a static indoor experience, the unit could morph into a deep exploration of a local creek so students come to understand the impact of development on the creek and create solutions that meet both the human and natural needs of the place—all while integrating key vocabulary, concepts, and ideas. The Community as Classroom design principle allows learning to happen anytime and anywhere, and it expands the traditional definition of school.

The three core themes of agency, equity, and community are viewed through the lenses of understanding your community, building belonging, and investing in social capital. Later in this chapter, we describe core tools to support implementing the principle of Community as Classroom.

Understanding Your Community

A local population must have a strong understanding and knowledge of place to build and sustain a thriving community. As Jane Jacobs shared in *The Death and Life of Great American Cities* (1992),

> The more successfully a city mingles everyday diversity of uses and users in its everyday streets, the more successfully, casually (and economically) its people thereby enliven and support well-located parks that can thus give back grace and delight to their neighborhoods instead of vacuity. (p. 111)

With this in mind, a prerequisite to any place-based implementation in a school is for the adults in the school to build a better understanding of the structure, challenges, and opportunities within the community. All communities have something worth exploring and to be proud of, even if, at the surface level, that doesn't seem to be the case. Relationships and connections within a place or community can be vibrant, even if an economy seems to be dying.

As described in the action steps near the end of this chapter, you can begin by exploring open spaces in your community—parks, trails, or creeks that form the ecological components of a place. Read the local paper and community notices, talk to business owners and employees, and introduce yourself to the library staff (if the community has a library) and other public officials. Is there a local museum in town? If so, encourage students to reach out and see if there is an opportunity to help support its work.

A Museum Partnership

Taya, a middle school student from the Journeys School in Jackson, Wyoming, experienced Community as Classroom through a partnership her school formed with a local children's museum. The museum needed a new exhibit about the human body, and Taya's class took up the challenge to meet the community need. Over the course of six weeks, the students examined how current museum attendees used the space. They then built prototypes and created models and interpretive displays for both adults and children.

The end result: a fully functioning, useable community resource built by students and linked to content, skills, and standards—all of which met a need in the community. During the process, Taya commented, "This is hard—it actually will be on display to the public." This statement, in which Taya expressed some surprise at the potential impact of the project, reinforces a persistent and unfortunate premise regarding our schools: most of the time, students do not see what they are doing as important, and communities do not recognize the schools and their students as great assets to support community improvement and vitality.

Communities around the world, although vastly different in many ways, all contain ecological, cultural, and economic components. The more teachers understand their own place, the more possibilities will emerge (dig more deeply into ideas with the How-to Guide in Chapter 8). As you explore your place, you will begin to make core connections to individuals and organizations that can support your implementation of place-based education.

Further, teachers don't have to do this work on their own. Tapping into community members who can facilitate learning about place is pivotal. Experts in place-based education help educators learn more about a place and not shy away from diving deeper. These experts can unlock the power of place for learners.

Many educators are personally deeply immersed in place but don't take advantage of that immersion for learning purposes (for themselves or with their students). Others are seeking to engage in the community but feel there is a barrier to overcome. More and more we believe that museums and libraries—and, in fact, every civic center and space—will be seen as a place of learning. We hope this realization will increase the number of teachers who understand the utility of place.

For students, learning happens every minute of every day. Although the modern school in the United States constrains "formal" learning to 6 or so hours a day over 10 months of the year, place-based education recognizes that the entire community is a year-round classroom experience. Whether bringing students into the community or bringing the community into the classroom, recognizing out-of-school experiences as valid learning experiences and actively building school-community partnerships increase student engagement and outcomes (Christenson, 2013).

Building Belonging

Highly functioning communities, regions, and countries rely on strong foundations in contributory citizenship and enterprise. As students see that they are valued members of the community, they also begin to see the role they could play as adults: as an employee, a citizen, a parent, or a volunteer. The increase in agency that develops through these partnerships helps students believe that they belong and are valued. Partnerships are key to building this capacity among students. Many great teachers find the right partners in the community to enhance learning in the classroom. A familiar example is the local fire station, which serves as a rich resource for early childhood learning about jobs in the community.

The school board can listen to presentations by elementary school students on how to improve playgrounds and consider the students' recommendations when planning for the future. High school students can partner with local government agencies to support the environmental analysis of a local creek as part of a larger development plan that is up for approval. Professionals in various fields, parents, teachers, and other community members can serve as mentors to help build a deep understanding that supports community well-being.

Specific community partnership programs can solidify and formalize relationships to reduce reliance and pressure on any one teacher. Teachers, students, and schools can understand and agree that the relationship will be reciprocal. For example, a public library in a small town may partner with the school to have students run a front-hall exhibit that rotates monthly. A community partnership program is an investment and agreement between the community and the school to provide authentic and expanded learning opportunities to all students in the school.

Local government agencies, nonprofits, businesses, and parks and forests all provide rich resources for an expanded view of the classroom. A community partnership program can formalize these relationships so they endure beyond a talented teacher or an engaged school leader. When a deeply embedded place-based education model is implemented, the community can pivot to see a school not just as a place to send their children but as an active, working component of the community. Students shift from waiting to contribute to actively participating. Peripheral service learning projects become meaningful parts of the learning experience. Every student contributes, interacts, and understands local communities and completes meaningful work.

Given time constraints, the community can also be brought into the classroom. Younger students can think about redesigning their classrooms as they develop skills in project planning, collaboration, mathematics, and the arts; older students can think about how larger schoolwide spaces—gardens, libraries, and hallways—could be used for authentic learning experiences that incorporate requisite knowledge and skills. The community can use these spaces for their activities and align them with learning goals students are working on.

The Boggs School seeks "to nurture a sense of place and develop a commitment to a better Detroit" (Boggs School, n.d. a). Students are immersed in local heritage, cultures, landscapes, opportunities, and experiences, using these as a foundation for the study of language arts, mathematics, social studies, science, and other subjects across the curriculum. Projects in the school and local community connect students and deepen their engagement and agency (Boggs School, n.d. b). For example, students honored neighborhood residents by celebrating their legacies with an exhibition of photos and stories. To produce the exhibition, students interviewed community members and researched local history. "This event created a powerful space that engendered the kind of education that is transformative, humanizing, community-centered, and nurturing of a beloved community" (De Palma, 2017, para. 5).

Investing in Social Capital

As students come to understand place, each of them brings a unique perspective along a broad continuum from positive to negative. Whereas one student sees the community as economically rich, another may see it as lacking in opportunity. Those who identify with a dominant or powerful population group may see equity and egalitarianism; those who are marginalized may see discrimination. Honest questions around perspective are integral to any place-based approach. As we build community as a classroom, all students must have equal access to the people, places, and organizations that serve as core elements of a community.

Equity builds as the definition of the classroom expands. The increasingly wide wealth-based opportunity gap (Shapiro, Meschede, & Osoro, 2013) seen in both the classroom and such out-of-school experiences as travel and access to museums and other cultural facilities decreases when place-based experiences are connected directly to the core learning program of the school. Because expectations encompass an expanded view of learning, the traditionally informal, out-of-school opportunities become embedded in the formal classroom, and social capital begins to develop more equitably among students. Social capital is the network of strong and weak ties held by any human (Fisher & Fisher, 2018). It builds over time as individuals develop increasingly more complex webs of relationships, as well as through intentional outreach, behaviors, and interactions that aren't always built into traditional learning environments.

Although the nature-versus-nurture debate about human development has converged into one that acknowledges the increasingly complex interaction between the two factors—fueled by the emerging field of epigenetics, which describes how genes get turned on and off based on the surrounding environment (Fisher, 2015)—the debate is missing the impact of privilege. With privilege comes social capital that a child inherits at birth. When the principle of Community as Classroom is well implemented, we level the playing field for students. Whether they are participating in internships, place-based projects, or other opportunities, students interact with a wide variety of adults from different fields, building strong and weak ties that increase their personal social capital. Students begin to build a view of a learning ecosystem where every interaction, organization, person, and location is a potential learning experience. When communities reciprocate and begin to see the school as a resource, everyone benefits. As students experience and interact with more adults and community organizations, teachers can help guide the development of professional habits. Students who build digital professional networks (such as through LinkedIn) develop contact lists and execute appropriate follow-up/thank you communication that will accelerate their building of social capital. Teachers can facilitate this development through intentional structures.

Finally, given the advances in technology and the significant increase in time that young (and old) people spend in the virtual world, the role of technology and virtual communities as classrooms must be acknowledged. These tools, although often a distraction, can be leveraged to better implement solutions to real-world challenges. For example, students at a high school in Hawai'i found out through an online social media platform that a local family needed new housing after a catastrophic storm. The students worked together to design a project (tied to their current objectives and standards) to build a house and support the family until they got back on their feet. Social technology enabled this authentic place-based project.

Implementation Methods and Approaches

Bringing in a guest speaker or having students investigate a local issue can quickly embed place into the learning experience. However, a few additional approaches can enrich that experience.

First, high-quality project-based learning (PBL) can provide structures to better organize the effort to implement Community as Classroom. Elements of PBL include a core "driving question"; a clear "need-to-know" objective that specifies the key knowledge and skills that students are expected to learn; an authentic audience; and a final product. For example, a core driving question might be "How does a lack of accessible transportation affect the economic well-being of a community?" A core driving question that is tied to a community need or issue helps make this connection. Project-based learning can be more effective in engaging students in comparison to a single guest speaker or disconnected field trip. (See Chapter 7 for more on project-based learning.)

Second, appropriately set leadership expectations and risk management practices. Just as students need to learn content, they also need to learn how to safely venture into, explore, and contribute to a place-based experience. Leadership skills, clear boundaries, and high expectations can help develop these capacities. For example, students should become well versed in understanding the human and environmental hazards that may be encountered. Human hazards include group management and behavior, whereas environmental hazards may be quickly moving water, city streets, crowds, or weather. Many students are also not accustomed to leading in classrooms. Skills such as communication, understanding leadership styles, and project planning all develop leadership capacities they will need.

Finally, "assessment *as* learning" rather than "assessment *of* learning" embeds authentic assessment into the experience itself. Unlike a final exam tacked onto the end of a unit, assessment as learning builds the authenticity of the experience. For example, rather than writing a paper and submitting it to a teacher for evaluation, students may present their findings to a local chamber of commerce, and their presentation becomes the assessment.

Teachers who use effective methods and approaches to support the Community as Classroom design principle are more likely to successfully implement it. Each of the methods and approaches described here builds capacity for students to understand the function of community and, eventually, become better citizens of future communities.

 **Cases**

The following examples illustrate how the Community as Classroom principle has been implemented by schools across the United States.

Hāna High and Elementary School: Hāna, Hawai'i

The vision of Hāna High and Elementary, known to locals as Hāna School, is *Ka'ike a ke kulanakauhale a pau he hei na ke keiki*, or "The knowledge of the whole village is absorbed by the child." As is common in Hawaiian culture, community and working together are keys to existence.

Learning at Hāna School incorporates the concepts of *'Ike Honua* (sense of place), *'Ike Mauli Lāhui* (cultural identity and a commitment to service), and *'Ike Kuana'ike* (perspective that honors all things past, present, and future) into learning. These are essential elements for students' engagement in their academic studies. Students experience place-based education from day one at Hāna School, whether it is learning on campus or in the community. Learning can happen anywhere and from anyone.

Long-time teacher Melody Cosma shares that the school's place-based, community-focused education "creates stronger roots. We had three double-hull canoes visit our community. We learned proper protocol to welcome people and [the] canoe (wa'a) [on the] Malama Honua Voyage. A former student, Nakua Lind, has become a captain for the *Hokulea*; [he] lives part-time in the community and returns each year to share knowledge he has with the student body."

Rick Rutiz leads Ma Ka Hāna Ka 'Ike, a nonprofit organization and vocational training program for at-risk youth. The organization, whose name is a motto that means "in working, one learns," has developed a special program in partnership with Hāna High and Elementary School. The program is designed to engage students in long-term place-based projects that focus on a student-identified community need or issue they address by building or creating something with their hands. The motto fuels all the projects students engage in.

In the Solar Monitoring Project, students monitor the input and output of the solar panels used in an off-grid solar classroom. For example, students realized that the community needed more sustainable energy options (more than 30 percent of the community is off-grid—that is, without access to publicly supplied electricity). They then worked with the University of Hawai'i to monitor the classroom's energy usage.

In another project, students planted 2,000 stalks of taro (a starchy root vegetable that is an important food staple in the area) in a land division called Wailua Nui. The planting is expected to yield up to an estimated 10,000 pounds of taro. These efforts were shared with other area farmers in hopes of restoring the streams and the *lo'i* (taro patches) they supply.

In 2019, Hāna High and Elementary School established a project-based learning cohort of 16 self-identified students who did not think traditional learning methods fit their educational needs. The school partnered with Ma Ka Hāna Ka 'Ike's building program and their community apprentice teachers to develop a multidisciplinary approach to learning that better fit students' needs. This concept was born out of a meeting with education philanthropist and school reform advocate Ted Dintersmith in Hāna. It was then developed into a complexwide initiative that could have an effect statewide in the future.

Hāna High and Elementary School is a powerful example of how the community can become the classroom, especially when it comes to understanding the culture, opportunities, and issues within those communities and places.

Hartford Heritage Project at Capital Community College: Hartford, Connecticut

Led by Jeffrey Partridge, professor of English and chair of the Department of Humanities at Capital Community College (CCC), the work being done in Hartford is a great example of providing students with new perspectives on access and opportunities within a city through place-based education (Hartford Heritage Project, n.d.). With the help of a National Endowment for the Humanities grant awarded in 2011, the college has gradually developed place-based methods in many of its courses.

Students who attend CCC are predominantly residents of Hartford, and more than 80 percent are eligible for Pell Grants. Black and Hispanic students make up 70 percent of the student population; 70 percent of students are female, and many identify as being single mothers. Forty to fifty languages are spoken among the students at CCC.

According to Partridge, "Students begin to see that Hartford—the place where they go to college and where many of them reside—is a vibrant place with a fascinating history that is part of their own heritage. Hartford is their city and they can and should be active participants in its future" (personal communication).

Capital Community College students now have the opportunity to experience and feel at home in places like museums and theaters in Hartford—places they would be unlikely to visit on their own because of cost or perceptions of exclusivity. Partridge and his colleagues have had to navigate a common belief among students that cultural places in particular are not "their space." Exposing students to theater and to museums in the context of college classes often leads to a deeper level of conversation about place and equity, access, privilege, and identity. In post-course evaluations and surveys, a majority of students typically report a greater sense of connectedness and belonging to their city, and a greater appreciation of its value.

Particularly in postsecondary education, we often neglect where students come from and focus on predetermined material and course objectives. The Hartford Heritage Project is a premier example of how to situate college-level learning in the context of communities in order to stimulate learning, engagement, and pride of place.

Círculos: Santa Ana, California

In 2017, Daniel Allen and Wes Krisel (and their team, including the coordinator Jessica Salcedo), two administrators in the Santa Ana Unified School District (SAUSD) in California, won a grant from XQ, an organization dedicated to reimagining high school education in the United States. The grant supported their commitment to embedding learning into the community and engaging students in a way that builds on their place-based strengths (Vander Ark, 2018e, para. 5). It led to the creation of the Círculos Advanced Learning Academy.

Círculos is developing a student-centered culture that features a strong peer-to-peer support system, connections with a circle of local mentors, and a commitment to place-based learning. Much of their student learning occurs outside the classroom, as students make frequent visits to local museums, businesses, nonprofits, and community organizations to broaden the scope of their education. At Círculos, every student is part of a tight-knit learning circle of peers, teachers, and community members (XQ, n.d. a).

In a 2017 blog post, Allen shared his thoughts about the design of Círculos:

> We wanted a school that could blend state of the art instructional practices with an authentic connection to the values and identity of our community. From using a Spanish name to integrating community partners to incorporating circle discussion practices and protocols, Círculos is a school that reflects the tremendous assets of our Santa Ana community. (para. 2)

He also elaborated on the central principle of Círculos—place:

> Círculos [has] no central campus. This is the statement that brings the ambition and unorthodox nature of the school into sharpest focus. School no longer occurs primarily within a building we call a school. We take the community and world around us as our canvas for learning. Círculos aspires to offer one of the most ambitious place-based learning environments in the country. (2017, para. 7)

Students work in project teams to address and study issues in their community that they care about. They work alongside community members in Santa Ana to improve or address whatever issue it is they are working on. Throughout their place-based projects, they have mentors, experts, and guides to help.

 ## Take Action

As teachers, we can take action toward building community as classroom. The following are steps you might consider and examples of the Community as Classroom principle as implemented by schools across the United States:

☐ **Explore your own place with family and friends.** Ask yourself the following questions: Who lives here now? Who lived here before? What drives the economy of this place? What are the ecological and geological systems at work in this place? Who holds power in this community? What are the current political issues? Is there inequity in this place?

☐ **Build a community map in your classroom or school.** Students of all ages can build community maps and add to them over multiple years. Specifying the location of projects, great partnerships, and community assets can remind teachers and students of community potential.

☐ **Create a community partnership program.** Begin by creating a formal document that outlines the benefits the organization will have by partnering with the school, and vice versa (see Figure 2.2 for an example). Identify your strongest informal partners and ask one of them to act as a pilot community partner. Include them in school communications, share annual results, and celebrate successful projects. Over time, you will build more partners interested in investing in students' learning experience.

☐ **Survey your parent body for "challenges worth addressing."** Create a brief survey to send to parents or community members to discover community needs. Post the results in the classroom or in a larger school space, and check off those challenges that the class has

FIGURE 2.2. **Sample Agreement for a Community Partner Program Agreement**

School Contact:
Partner Organization:
Partner Contact:
Project Name: Sustainable Events Project
Project Goal(s): A local community foundation runs an annual event that includes a community meal, fun run, and exhibition booths. As part of the commitment to sustainability, the foundation needs a way to measure the carbon footprint of the event. The goal of the project is to measure and report on the annual carbon footprint of the event.
School Commitments: As a school (specifically, a 10th grade math class), we commit to the following: • Collecting data during the event • Analyzing the data • Translating the data into carbon-footprint metrics • Reporting back to the organization in both presentation and written form
Partner Commitments: As a community partner, we commit to the following: • Providing an introductory presentation to students to describe the background and need (1 hour) • Providing access to required data or contacts to access the data • Acknowledging the student contribution in a press release or other media releases • Reviewing a draft of the project and providing initial feedback (1 hour) • Meeting with students at school at the end of the project to review their report and provide feedback (1 hour)
Signatures: _____ Project leader (school):   _____ Project liaison (partner organization):   _____

addressed. Repeat the process annually to expand the list of potential projects.

☐ **Take your students out of the classroom.** Start simply. Take them on a walking tour of the school to observe the economic, ecological, and cultural components. Build leadership capacity from the start by asking students what leaving the classroom should look like and how they want to represent themselves. End by having students brainstorm potential opportunities for place-based experiences that exist within the school building or campus.

☐ **Write a digital community newspaper with your students.** Simple digital tools such as the online media platforms Medium and Blogger make it easy to create and post news stories. Students can move beyond the typical classroom paper to write real articles about real issues in the community and make them public from the start. The authenticity will matter to students, and the resource, especially in smaller towns where local newspapers are no longer sustainable, could be welcomed.

❑ **Visit local historical sites.** Boston Public Schools has created place-based resources that help educators when they are exploring local historical sites (BPS Place-Based Learning, n.d.). Schools have started to move beyond typical field trips and incorporate more ongoing place-based experiences.

❑ **Do a community deep dive.** At Teton Science Schools in northwest Wyoming and eastern Idaho, high school students look through the lens of the Place Triangle (Figure 2.1, p. 23) to understand community sustainability. They complete a deep-dive inquiry into the issue using an approach that integrates social studies, science, economics, visual arts, and English.

❑ **Take advantage of internships.** Students enrolled in the national network of Big Picture Learning schools are out in internships with adults two full days a week, implementing the Community as Classroom principle. The experience builds social capital along with a host of other knowledge, skills, and dispositions (Big Picture Learning, n.d.).

❑ **Consider joint facilities.** e3 Civic High and the downtown San Diego Central Library are housed in the same building; the library and community are brought directly to the school, and vice versa. The Math and Science Institute, a high school in Tacoma, Washington, is located within the Point Defiance Zoo and Aquarium. Students engage in place-based projects around zoology. Here are a few additional examples of joint facilities:

— Houston A+ Unlimited Potential is located inside the Houston Museum of Natural Science. Students regularly engage with museumgoers (as docents) and workers (by collaborating on exhibit design).

— Gary Comer College Prep, a high school in Chicago's Noble Network, located with a youth center, has rooftop gardens and community gardens across the street.

— Thrive Public Schools' new K–8 campus in the Linda Vista neighborhood of San Diego is located with the Bayside Community Center.

— Roscoe Independent School District in Texas hosts businesses within the district's high school building, including businesses providing drone technology and veterinary services.

Learning Sciences Connection

The study of how people learn, more formally named "learning sciences," provides us with research that supports the place-based design principle and ideas discussed in this chapter. For more information, read *Designing for Learning* (Charlot et al., 2018). See also Figures 0.4 and 0.5 (pp. 7–8) in the Introduction. The Community as Classroom principle aligns with the following learning science principles:

- Cognition: 3
- Motivation: 7
- Identity: 12
- Individual Variability: 14

3

Learner-Centered

We support young people in finding their niche and stance in the world. People always ask, what is your secret sauce? It consists of four ingredients. The first is pay attention to the whole student. Pay attention to their strengths, interests, passions, curiosities, fears, communities, and their families . . . We have noticed that those moments when a young person realizes that what he or she is learning in school connects to something they are passionate about in the real world, the rigor will be there, you can push deeply and the level of engagement that you see in young people will take off.

—**Carlos Moreno,** Chief Executive Officer, Big Picture Learning

Outside regular school hours, Jemar Lee is seen more as a community activist, spokesperson, and architect than a typical high school student. He is a graduate of the Iowa BIG school, a learner-centered school that provides students with ongoing place-based experiences (Getting Smart Staff, 2019, para. 1).

Before attending Iowa BIG, Jemar was disenchanted by learning and felt trapped within the four walls of his school. Particularly as a middle school student, he was struggling to find relevance and autonomy in a more traditional setting and was constantly getting reprimanded and suspended for expressing his disinterest. "I felt trapped and was without purpose. There wasn't a place for me and my interests at the school. Everything was preset." Once he was at Iowa BIG, that all changed.

After one pivotal moment and a final outcry to his principal for a change and a learning model that better fit his needs, Jemar was offered the choice to stay at his current school (with an amended schedule), attend the local alternative school, or go to Iowa BIG. He didn't know much about Iowa BIG but decided to check it out. After visiting, he realized it was different; it was a place where he could learn and contribute.

Iowa BIG's innovative design won XQ and Next Generation Learning Challenge grants. Cedar Rapids–area school districts, businesses, and non-profit partners came together to provide a unique learning experiences for high school students.

Students spend some time at their sending high school but most of it at Iowa BIG. Students engage in community-connected interdisciplinary projects that result in rigorous real-world learning for students across the region. Students select from a group of interdisciplinary projects that were designed by teachers, students, and partners to address local issues and meet state standards. The community sees young people as assets, and young people see themselves as meaningful contributors to the community (XQ, n.d. b).

During his time at Iowa BIG, which is located in a coworking space in downtown Cedar Rapids, Jemar accomplished a lot, to say the least. Among other achievements, he created a nonprofit, drew a new floor plan for the school, and partnered with the city of Cedar Rapids to redesign a farm zoo.

"The first project I did at Iowa BIG focused around my passions—architecture and interior design," explained Jemar. At the time, the school was exploring design concepts for a brand-new space. Jemar continued,

> I was given the opportunity to create a floor plan that would accommodate all Iowa BIG learners and staff. After a lot of research and putting my knowledge and skills to the test, I presented my design to the building owner and manager. My design was not only taken into consideration, but it was actually fully implemented! (Convergence, 2018)

"Iowa BIG is impacting our economic development," Jemar points out. "Students are staying here in Iowa now because they have these connections" (Getting Smart Staff, 2019).

Jemar worked both within and outside the school walls to develop meaningful projects that interested him, tapped into his strengths, and challenged him to grow his own skill set. These experiences helped him develop a greater sense of agency and purpose in his life and work.

"My days of looking at white walls, white paper, and listening to colorless lectures would [soon] be over," said Jemar (Lee, 2017, para. 8). "I would be learning out in the community or within a dynamic working space that invited collaboration. Every day, I would be doing something with a purpose!"

"Learner-centered education is where I get to be myself and find ownership of something in my community—that opens doors for my voice," said Jemar.

The Principle: Learner-Centered

Learner-centered education, comprising experiences like those Jemar experienced at Iowa BIG, represents a paradigm shift from what we could term a more conventional "school-centered" approach to education. The idea that we should focus on the individual student is not new, but for decades modern education systems have focused on the school rather than the learner. As far back as constructivist lab schools and the work of John Dewey, educators realized that students need to feel connected to what they were learning and that their voice and interests mattered. The following quote from Dewey (n.d./1907) makes the point:

> From the standpoint of the child, the great waste in the school comes from his inability to utilize the experiences he gets outside the school in any complete and free way within the school itself; while, on the other hand, he is unable to apply in daily life what he is learning at school. That is the isolation of the school—its isolation from life. When the child gets into the schoolroom he has to put out of his mind a large part of the ideas, interests, and activities that predominate in his home and neighborhood. So the school, being unable to utilize this everyday experience, sets painfully to work, on another tack and by a variety of means, to arouse in the child an interest in school studies.

Education Reimagined, a national nonprofit, states, "Learner-centered education is about an entirely new way of seeing, thinking about, and acting on education" (see www.education-reimagined.org). It suggests a focus on three key aspects of the learner:

1. Each learner is seen as being unique in meaningful ways. They have unique backgrounds, circumstances, and starting points with unique strengths, challenges, interests, and aspirations. All of these unique attributes call for unique responses from their learning system.

2. Each learner is seen as having unbounded potential—potential that will unfold at its own pace and in its own way. Every single learner is a wonder to behold.

3. Each learner is seen as having an innate desire to learn. The job of the education system is to unleash that desire.

Education Reimagined also provides what it calls a "North Star for Learner-Centered Education," consisting of five elements of effective learner-centered communities: learner agency; socially embedded; personalized, relevant, and contextualized; open-walled; and competency-based (see Figure 3.1). Place-based education incorporates each of these elements.

Learner-Centered is a key design principle of place-based education, and it embodies the notion of learner agency—the ability to act on the world

FIGURE 3.1. The Five Elements: A North Star for Learner-Centered Education

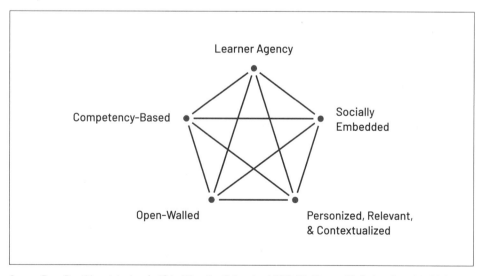

Source: From *Practitioner's Lexicon* (p. 5), by Education Reimagined, 2018, Washington DC: Author. Copyright 2018 by Education Reimagined. Reprinted with permission.

(as described in Chapter 1). In learner-centered environments, students see themselves in the learning, and facilitators are able to design experiences with and for each student. As a result, students are getting what they need as individuals, starting with "who" and "where" they are in the learning journey.

Unlike school-confined learning, place-based education allows for infinitely more opportunities to bring elements of learners' identity to their learning and experiences, to help unleash their potential in a way that taps into their strengths and is authentic and more equitable. This powerful combination of learner-centered education and place-based experience unleashes student agency and purpose.

Learner-centered education is also socially embedded—that is, student experiences are connected to social contexts and communities, through place and in working with others. It also is open-walled—that is, "learning happens at many times and in many places and intentionally leverages its expansive nature in the learner's development of competencies. It creates and takes full advantage of opportunities in a variety of communities, settings, times, and formats" (Convergence, 2018, p. 8).

Traditional education settings often limit the connections that students can make to how the learning fits within their world outside school. By contrast, learner-centered, socially embedded experiences provide meaning and context for students, resulting in deeper learning.

Learner-centered education is also usually competency-based—that is, students demonstrate mastery by showing what they know and how they have progressed. This approach allows students to learn not only at their own pace but also in their own way. For example, Jemar's architecture project (described earlier in this chapter) could be a way to learn and demonstrate a set of math competencies. A report about the project could help fulfill requirements related to writing competencies, and a public presentation would add evidence of oral communication competencies.

A competency-based system allows students to learn and demonstrate growth and agency in unique ways. It requires extra work

> "If we want to be student-centered, I suggest we start where students are productively learning—outside of school at the edges, mingling with people they want to learn from, inventing, discovering, creating, and seeking to understand."
>
> **—Elliot Washor,**
> cofounder, Big Picture Learning (2018, para. 3)

for teachers in terms of building competencies into projects and helping individual students and teams connect with the community, but the payoff is the increase in motivation that comes from students' sense that what they are doing is relevant. (See more on competency-based systems in Chapter 8.)

Health Leadership High School in Albuquerque, New Mexico, is a good example of a competency-based system. The school helps young people contribute to community health and prepare for leadership roles in healthcare. "We don't have classes," said Executive Director Blanca López. "We have projects. Most students work on three per day. It's the main focus of the school" (Vander Ark, 2018b, para. 3).

Each summer, the staff solicits project ideas from community health providers. The outreach results in project partners for students and real-time opportunities. Each project plan includes desired outcomes—for the community and for the students. Every project must have deliverables that are valuable to the community, explained López. "We see where needs are. We create advocates for change."

Health Leadership students also participate in paid internships. Teachers can map important competencies to both team projects and individual internships. Each learner may have a unique learning journey, but they all have the opportunity to develop and demonstrate important skills.

Competency-based learning unlocks the opportunities that place-based education can bring, and vice versa. For almost two decades, Chugach School District in Alaska has been working toward implementing more learner-centered practices—specifically, competency-based education and tying learning to place. One of the ways in which they have done this is through having students "own" their competency-based learning journeys (Education Reimagined, n.d., para. 2). This approach includes involving students in conversations about who they are, and how and what they want to learn every step of the way. The district also started using performance-based assessments to get a deeper level of understanding of what students know and are able to do. The connection to place? These competencies and performance-based assessments are often tied to the opportunities, challenges, culture, or history of students' local and broader communities in Alaska.

As evidenced by many credit recovery systems, it is possible to offer competency-based learning opportunities that are not connected to the community and that risk becoming nothing more than a checklist void of relevance. Connections to place through projects and internships take more work than logging in to an online system; but in addition to developing desired academic competencies, they promote deeper learning, agency, and an entrepreneurial mindset.

Remake Learning (n.d.), a Pittsburgh nonprofit "that ignites engaging, relevant, and equitable learning practices in support of young people navigating rapid social and technological change," supports open-walled experiences in six regional educational ecosystems. One aim of the organization is that the learning environments will "connect all the places learners live, work, and play, including schools, libraries, museums, parks, clubs, community centers, centers of faith, at home, and online" (Remake Learning, n.d., para. 19). Held in April or May each year, Remake Learning Days provide a week of activities that help schools get started with place-based learning.

From Delivering Content to Coconstructing and Facilitating Learning

On traditional field trips, we often ask all participating students to engage with a place in the same way. Katie Martin, in her book *Learner-Centered Innovation* (2018), writes that we must make the shift from delivering content to a cohort of learners—with everyone engaging together and asking the same questions leading to the same final product or outcome—to providing opportunities for individual students to engage and apply what they learn in authentic scenarios and places.

Educators who are not from the same communities or places that their students are from may shy away from engaging in place. Often, they neglect to include certain content or places in their teaching because they themselves aren't familiar with the locations or communities. This reluctance or neglect could potentially inhibit learning opportunities and connections that might otherwise be made. Once educators' mindsets shift to being coconstructors and learners alongside students, the need to be the bearer of all the knowledge can be replaced with the gift of facilitating and engaging in the learning process.

Further, ignoring the importance of place can limit an educator's understanding of students' strengths and social capital. Students' experiences are not alike, nor are their backgrounds. If we take a learner-centered approach and embed place in experiences, we are bound to find out more about who students are, what rich assets they bring to our classrooms, and how we might better connect them to their passions and interests within their communities. A learner-centered approach makes it clear that we want to create more equitable environments for everyone, not just laud test scores and disregard the individuals students are.

Place enables educators to shift from delivering content to facilitating learning in many possible ways. It is a useful vehicle for teachers and students to experience new and novel situations together, increasing equity, agency, and community, and focusing on each individual learners' goals, needs, interests, and dreams.

On Personalization

As discussed in Chapter 1, personalized learning has become a popular theme in education in the United States, but it is usually applied to skill building. With the learner-centered lens, personalized learning focuses on individual student growth, development of agency, and boosting access and opportunity for each student (Getting Smart Staff, with eduInnovation and Teton Science Schools, 2017, p. 2). In other words, students have more control over the time, place, path, and pace of learning. When learning is more personalized, content and skill development becomes more relevant and appropriate for the individual learner. Place-based experiences can help develop a fuller sense of identity, which leads to student agency.

School typically embodies a defined set of outcomes to be achieved on a pre-determined path, but that approach often comes with a diminished sense of self and motivation. Personalization happens when students feel they are advancing in their expertise, when they can reflect and observe their own growth through a set of experiences and products rather than a checklist of skills covered.

Personalized learning sets up place-based education with personalized "on-ramps." For example, Cristo Rey schools, a network of high schools in more than 20 states, offer weekly work-study experiences for their students. A personalized on-ramp before an experience might begin with a teacher telling students something like this: "Next week, we are going to the park to do some data collection. Some of you need to improve your data-collection skills before next week so you will be ready to fully participate." In this way, a personalized on-ramp can help a student succeed within a whole-group project. Goal setting and reflection are key to personalized goals and skill development.

 ## Cases

The following examples illustrate how the Learner-Centered design principle has been implemented in schools across the United States.

Del Lago Academy: Escondido, California

The founding principal of Del Lago Academy, Keith Nuthall, says the intent and design of the school derive from the beliefs that the student population is representative of the immediate community and that learning is centered on the students. This public high school serves about 800 students and is focused on applied sciences. Although science is a core part of the teaching and learning, the school puts just as much focus on students doing rich interdisciplinary projects.

Students at Del Lago work across disciplines to problem solve, think creatively, and create their own meaningful solutions. District science lead and founding teacher Alec Barron wants students not only to have desirable skills and knowledge for potential employers but also to be doing meaningful work inside and outside the physical school building—work that feels relevant and connects to their lives now.

Students intern at local companies (many of them biotech companies) and hospitals, including one less than a half-mile away. Their interdisciplinary projects relate to the work that they are doing in their internships. Mentors and partners at the internships often inform students and Del Lago educators about what students need to know and what would be helpful for them to be learning while in high school.

Students are doing socially embedded, open-walled, personalized, and competency-based work at Del Lago. They are responsible for uploading evidence of their work to a digital portfolio as a way to earn a digital badge and demonstrate the competencies they are individually working on. The students use the badges to show intern partners or future employers what they know, believe, and are able to do. Students can upload photos and videos to demonstrate their science competencies, and they are also required to write about and reflect on their learning.

Explaining Del Lago's use of digital badges, Barron (2017) said this:

> It creates opportunities for learners to be engaged in a larger community of practice. Mentors can provide feedback on formative artifacts that will become evidence used to earn a badge. Also, this allows artifacts of skills, knowledge and dispositions to be used across multiple digital badges. This helps illuminate the interconnections between digital badges and prevent the compartmentalization of skills and knowledge. (para. 9)

Dr. Edward Abeyta, K–12 outreach lead for the University of California–San Diego, shared more about Barron as a leader: "Barron is a leader in education who is leveraging digital badging as a means to honor student learning inside and outside of the classroom by allowing students to showcase their competencies to future employers" (Vander Ark, 2018a, para. 13).

ACE Leadership High School: Albuquerque, New Mexico

Northwest of downtown Albuquerque, there is a high school of about 400 students, ranging in ages from 14 to 20. ACE Leadership High School primarily serves students who have already dropped out or seemingly were on their way to dropping out of high school. (Much of this section is drawn from the results of our case study with this school [Getting Smart, 2018a].) On average, students at ACE have been enrolled in three or more high schools and frequently claim that school wasn't working for them. Many hold jobs, sometimes even two, and typically come from low socioeconomic backgrounds.

The founders of ACE knew that students didn't need more of the same type of traditional learning, but they needed to be more learner-centered and to provide students with authentic and truly meaningful learning experiences.

At ACE, students engage daily in two ongoing interdisciplinary place-based projects, resulting in about eight complete long-term projects over the course of a year. Each project has intentional direct connections to industries in the local area or community. Students experiences ebb in and out of learning spaces both at ACE and in the community, working with peers at different stages of their Transition Ladder (Apprentice 1, Apprentice 2, Journeyman/Journeywoman, Final Year Student, and Alumni). Their transitions are measured by competencies—not by end-of-year exams or summative tests.

Projects at ACE always have a tie to a real-world need and are usually initiated by a student-generated driving question, creating a greater sense of student agency and investment in the work. Students also have to work directly with an industry partner or client. Students work for extended periods of time investigating driving questions and working to create (often with their hands) a product or solution that meets specific industry requirements and client needs. Past place-based projects include designing foot bridges, rebuilding local skate parks, and designing the layout for a zoo. Before students present such projects, they talk about their work to clients with whom they're collaborating and often with other professionals in the community. Their work is socially embedded.

"A great example of this is during a place-based project where students literally went to the Albuquerque Department of Transportation (DoT) to share their thoughts on a proposed public transit system that was intended to serve the working class community," said Lucy Alfonso, a lead teacher at ACE. "Students knew the proposed route wasn't going to serve those who used public transit most, so they designed a better system that ran along routes that would serve those in most need and then presented these plans to the DoT."

 ## Take Action

As teachers, we can take action toward building learner-centered environments. The following are steps you might consider and examples of the Learner-Centered design principle as implemented by schools across the United States:

☐ **Encourage leadership opportunities and student-formed committees.** When immersed in a sense of place, students start to feel strong conviction and connections to causes or issues in their communities or elsewhere. They latch on to causes they care about and initiatives that matter most to them and their communities. Student-formed committees and leadership opportunities are a great way to deepen student engagement and motivation. Students lead the board of directors at the nonprofit organization One Stone in Boise, Idaho, and have created their own committees based on projects tied to local challenges.

☐ **Conduct student-led conferences.** Teacher-student conferences that are actually led by the student are a great way to get started with learner-centered practices, and they can reveal key insights about our teaching as well. Student-led conferences can reveal where needs are and are not being met, how a student likes to learn, and where there are opportunities for growth. They also provide an opportunity for students to divulge place-based experiences they've had that made an impact on them, as well as those that they'd like to have. When students share their thoughts about their learning, engagement increases—as well as ownership and agency.

☐ **Use competency-based report cards.** Redesign learning around competencies and incorporate them into student report cards. Many schools are using portfolios in conjunction with mastery-based transcripts. Check out the website of the Mastery Transcript Consortium (https://mastery.org), a network of schools that are working together to create "a high school transcript that reflects the unique skills, strengths, and interests of each learner" (Mastery Transcript Consortium, n.d.).

☐ **Create a "genius hour."** Well established in many schools, a genius hour is a time for students to explore any topic, in any way. Create a high level of accountability by linking the explorations to the set of skills required by the school—especially those related to collaboration, communication, and creativity.

☐ **Make daily goals and reflection a habit.** Build a habit of students writing daily goals around standards or learning targets and reflecting on those goals. Over time, they will easily answer the questions "Where have I learned?" "What am I learning?" and "What am I learning next?"

☐ **Move toward more self-directed learning.** At New Harmony High School in New Orleans, the school's vision statement emphasizes place and learner-centeredness in its opening sentences: "New Harmony High School empowers each student to actively direct their own learning. As our name suggests, students will work to find new harmonies in order to restore balance that has been lost in our coastal communities, finding new ways of sustaining ourselves in an uncertain future" (New Harmony High School, n.d., para. 1). They simply state, "School is Everywhere." Students engage in projects that connect them to their community. They view most projects through the lens of what is going on in the coastal region and what is being done to preserve the land. In addition to their teachers, students work alongside community members, mentors, and local experts.

Learning Sciences Connection

The study of how people learn, more formally named "learning sciences," provides us with research that supports the place-based design principle and ideas discussed in this chapter.

For more information, read *Designing for Learning* (Charlot et al., 2018). See also Figures 0.4 and 0.5 (pp. 7–8) in the Introduction. The Learner-Centered design principle aligns with the following learning sciences principles:

- Cognition: 2
- Motivation: 8, 9
- Identity: 11
- Individual Variability: 14, 15, 16

4

Inquiry-Based

I think we don't know ourselves until we know the world around us and how we connect to that world.

—**Laura Haspela,** educator

Science Leadership Academy (SLA) sits in the heart of Center City Philadelphia, surrounded by old brick buildings and local markets that serve as hangouts for students, juxtaposed with new condominiums and boutique grocery stores. The physical and structural changes in this rapidly gentrifying neighborhood are not the only transformations happening here, because at SLA, students' minds and hearts are evolving daily.

Horace, a junior, became involved in education reform when he stepped into SLA. He lives around the corner from the school and has seen the changes that are happening in his community. He spends most of his time downtown, living the life of a teenager but also engaging in essential conversations about improving his city. Poised, thoughtful, and articulate—and only 17 years old—Horace is a youth commissioner for the city of Philadelphia, city director of a nonprofit organization, and a vocal advocate for his school. His work is deeply entrenched in place—particularly around inquiring and investigating what has come before, what is happening now, and how he can better serve his community in the future.

How did Horace—who in elementary school was self-reportedly "an average student"—get to where he is today? One explanation is that his teachers know the importance of place. They incorporate deep inquiry into every project students do. Without this deep inquiry-based environment, Horace says, he doesn't know if he would have accomplished what he has so far. It is inquiry—a form of active learning in which students identify and pose questions for extended exploration in their classroom—that drove him to be dedicated to his schooling and revealed his passions and interests.

 ## The Principle: Inquiry-Based

Inquiry-based learning is grounded in observing, asking relevant questions, making predictions, and collecting relevant data to understand the economic, ecological, social-political, and cultural elements of a community—from local to global. The inquiry-based approach develops curiosity, wonder, and a methodical approach for students to understand their place in their world (Colburn, 2000).

By developing contextualized and personalized questions for inquiry, students will develop acuity as lifelong learners. They harbor a constant inquisitiveness that will increase their engagement not only in learning but also with their surroundings.

Inquiry is deeply connected to the Learner-Centered principle described in Chapter 3. As students take more control over the direction of the learning experience through a methodical and rigorous process and design thinking, they begin to see areas where they could create local solutions to discovered challenges. Nate shares how inquiry has become integral to his life and process as an educator:

> When I came to Teton Science Schools in the '90s, I was very focused just on science. Now when I drive through any community or those [where] I grew up, I am always asking myself questions about the community. Now I ask, "Where does this river go? Who was here before?" My inquiry level has gone up dramatically as I think about those things. I want to figure out what is going on in those communities and find aspects unique to those places.

Inquiry is a natural process for the human species and helps us develop a deep understanding of community. The human brain is designed to take in external stimuli and ask questions about how to interpret them. From birth, babies engage in the inquiry process through a cause-and-effect approach: *if I do this, then this will happen*. All young people have this natural propensity to wonder, but as a result of traditional schooling and increased responsibilities, adults' levels of awe and wonder tend to decline. The premise of inquiry is to help instill in learners a sense of wonder they will carry with them throughout their lives.

Inquiry, although well known in the sciences and heavily promoted through schools' adoption of the Next Generation Science Standards, is a relevant approach for all disciplines. Students make observations about the world around them to help articulate good questions. From the questions, students hypothesize about the outcomes. Rather than offering random guesses, students look at background knowledge to understand the topic fully before making a hypothesis. They design methodology to help answer the question and subsequently collect data to help make conclusions around the hypothesis. Students then summarize data through results and analysis and articulate conclusions around whether the data supported the hypothesis. Finally, they share their conclusions and make new observations.

Each of these steps can be used in isolation to deepen understanding. Students in math classes can start each day with a photo or object and a prompt to create good questions that they subsequently share along with a hypothesis. High school science classes can look at a relevant news story on air quality in their area and create a quick methodology for collecting relevant data. Preschoolers might observe plants growing in their classroom and ask questions about some aspect they are curious about. Elementary-level social studies students might look at the amount of recyclable material that is thrown away in their room and chart the data over a period of time to practice different data collection methods.

Each step of the inquiry process is useful in itself, and over time, inquiry becomes second nature to well-practiced students. A student recently reported to her parents, "Science was great today. The teacher gave us the topic, and we designed and carried out our own experiments." Students are active, engaged, and in control of their learning through the inquiry-based approach.

Levels of Inquiry

Banchi and Bell (2008) articulate four levels of inquiry—confirmation, structured, guided, and open—to help support implementation with students who have varying amounts of experience and skill. By allowing a student to determine one or more elements of the inquiry process, the inquiry becomes increasingly learner-centered—and requires more experience and skill by the student, as well as the teacher, to implement.

When the question, methods, and conclusion are all known, students are completing a *confirmation* inquiry. This is typically the case in introductory high school chemistry classrooms where safety and control are critical.

Structured inquiry occurs when the conclusions are unknown but the teacher determines the question and procedure. A teacher may allow students to choose which variables to change, but the procedure for each is established. Citizen science, in which classrooms partner with local agencies and universities to collect data, is often structured inquiry.

Guided inquiry releases control to the student around the methods—the teacher articulates the question and students come up with the methods and carry out the inquiry. This approach often occurs when a teacher or community member has a specific question that needs data to answer but has not developed the methodology to secure it.

Finally, *open* inquiry is fully designed by the student. The teacher may provide content guardrails, background knowledge, and learning goals, but the student, either individually or with others, completes the entire inquiry. As students develop more capacity for inquiry, agency increases. Students realize that their questions are important, relevant, and meaningful to both them and the community.

Because the sciences have advanced the inquiry process, people often equate it with the scientific method. By viewing the world through a scientific lens, students learn to ask better questions and critically analyze results that are collected by others.

Design thinking (the topic of Chapter 6) is directly connected to the inquiry approach. Whereas inquiry often only leads to suggestions or recommendations about next steps relevant to the conclusions, design thinking articulates a process that students can use to design and build the recommended solutions. The early stages of the design process include defining the challenge. Inquiry can be used to do just this.

Take, for example, a teacher who knows that she needs to cover water and political systems for her 7th grade science and social studies curricula, respectively. In the past, she assigned students to read relevant chapters in the district-provided textbooks, asked them to summarize their notes, and administered a test. Students spent class time taking notes and homework time reading ahead to prepare for the next class.

After recognizing that engagement and student performance were chronically low, the teacher imagined an inquiry approach to help students better understand the requisite knowledge and skills. Her unit started with students articulating what they knew and wanted to know about the two different topics. After some discussion around the scientific method, a water-quality comparison lab, and basic background readings on water, students designed their own inquiry about the water quality in a local stream. In small groups, they made observations, wrote predictions, and carried out student-designed methodology to collect data.

Simultaneously, they used inquiry to investigate local political systems by observing that there was a local debate about water quality, building predictions around citizen opinion, collecting data through parent surveys, and analyzing the results. With both these inquiries complete, students could then complete the larger project with more ownership and engagement than were evident in the previous iterations of the unit.

Inquiry and Authentic Learning

Through inquiry, students learn how to ask relevant questions to understand the world based on evidence and data. They pursue questions of interest and develop novel and complex learning experiences.

As students develop the tools of inquiry, they become "truth-seekers," asking their own questions and collecting their own data. Because their observations and questions vary based on their different backgrounds, environments, and cultures, each student can better seek his or her own truth through inquiry. By making observations relevant to their context, they connect the inquiry to what is important to them.

During the inquiry process, students evaluate the bias and error in their data. With progressively more experience, they become well equipped to collect primary data and evaluate second-hand information—whether news, social media, or statistical data.

Inquiry also provides students with practice in big-data analysis (i.e., with extremely large data sets). Data scientists and big-data engineers are among the fastest-growing occupations in the United States, and demand is outstripping supply (Columbus, 2017), but our schools and classrooms do not spend enough time preparing students for these occupations outside of traditional math classes. Repeated practice in collecting and analyzing original data can support the development of these skills.

Intrepid Academy at Hale is a joint venture between Boston Public Schools and Hale Reservation, a 1,137-acre recreational and educational facility. Students engage in inquiry and rigorous academics every day, spending time in nature and making connections as to why place is important to them. They investigate the humanities and "green chemistry" by exploring their natural surroundings with their peers in advisory groups and with a designated outdoor guide (InnovateBPS, n.d.). Students report that these experiences, including constructing their own questions and answers while outdoors, has helped build their social skills and ability to work as a team (Andrews, 2018).

Beyond the individual benefits, original inquiry can have a significant effect on others, as students research important community challenges that are of interest to them and, through design thinking, figure out how to make change happen. Examples of effects beyond the classroom include students creating a community map of water bottle–refilling stations, designating crosswalks in small towns, and building exhibits for local museums.

Why Inquiry Is Preferable to Other Instructional Approaches

Compare the inquiry approach to other, more direct and prescriptive approaches. When students are provided with an observation, a question, and a research methodology, they are deprived of the recognition that their context matters. Some, but frequently a minority, learn to follow directions and "do school" well, whereas others must struggle because they lack comprehension, interest, or context—or all three. Too many students are left behind, disengaged or disinterested. Those who succeed in this learning environment may become great at following rules but poor at developing creative ways to seek the truth.

A commitment to inquiry within place-based education allows for a true exploration of novel and complex problems. Discussing water scarcity in the world via a textbook page leads to far lower engagement and fewer successful outcomes than if students had to answer the question "What is our per capita daily water use in the school, and how does it compare to that of schools in other locations around the globe?" The latter approach engages the innate curiosity in each student, whereas the former leads to disengagement for many. Complexity and novelty emerge with an open level of inquiry, as described earlier. This does not mean that authentic assessment and individual accountability are lacking in other approaches, but it does mean that the real, long-term outcome may be unknown to the teacher and students.

Finally, inquiry helps to build equity. All community members need the tools to properly digest, filter, analyze, and understand meaningful data. An uninformed portion of the population degrades the sense of ownership that individuals need in a participatory democracy. Evidence suggests that students have a difficult time evaluating validity in the news and on the Internet (Stanford History Education Group, 2016)—yet the integrity of democracy and community depend on this skill. The responsibility lies on us as teachers to ensure that every student in every school has the inquiry skills necessary to understand an increasingly complex world.

Being equipped and prepared for an inquiry-based approach does not happen all at once. But methodical skill development and change management practices can produce a paradigm shift for both teacher and students.

 # Cases

The following examples illustrate how the Inquiry-Based principle has been implemented by schools across the United States.

Cottonwood School for Civics and Science: Portland, Oregon: The Library Project

The 1st and 2nd grade students began by constructing three-dimensional maps of an imaginary neighborhood, including people, buildings, streets, and transportation. Students then set out in their own neighborhood to learn more about the essential features. On their forays, they toured a bank, an apartment building, the tram that connects the South Waterfront district with the campus of the Oregon Health and Science University, a fire department, the central library, and local parks. They rode the streetcar and learned more about safely walking the city sidewalks. Additionally, a Portland police officer visited the classrooms and a local resident talked to students about her family history and the future development of the South Waterfront.

Using the inquiry approach, students asked the people they met what *community* means to them. The answers helped build the students' own understanding of community. In the classroom, teachers shared books to support this learning and to provide diverse perspectives of children living in other urban areas.

After thoroughly exploring their neighborhood, students discovered that the South Waterfront neighborhood did not have a library. They decided to build a Little Free Library, which several students had seen in their home neighborhoods. A mechanical engineer from a construction company visited the classrooms to give a quick lesson on essential design features. Using the list of features, students came up with designs that the company's employees could use to build a library. Among other requests, students asked that the library be shaped like a house and have a glass door and a triangle-shaped roof with a chimney. The builders created a beautiful structure based on student drawings and brought it into the school for the children to paint. The library was installed in the South Waterfront and was opened for business.

High Tech High: San Diego, California: Colorado River Project

Working through a nonprofit organization called Blue Dot Education, Brian Delgado and Mike Strong, teachers at High Tech High, have helped students launch place-based inquiry projects. In the spring of 2018, they ran a mixed-age, semester-long immersive program called Semester Upstream, in which they supported 23 high school students in making a documentary film, *Heart of the West: A Student Exploration of the Colorado River Watershed.* Students read about, researched, discussed, and visited the river. They talked with members and leaders of the local communities that were affected by the management of the Colorado River.

In a video posted on Vimeo (Josephs, 2018a), Olivia Ho, student director of the documentary, shared her thoughts on this project:

> I think my initial goal, coming into the class and applying for the class, was to do something totally outside of my comfort zone . . . but after seeing the Salton Sea and seeing all of these sites and reading about it, it quickly became, like, I had a connection to this river and to this land and the people. I think that we need to save this river and help it out any way that we can. I don't think I knew our water came from the Colorado River. I just thought that the water came from the pipes and then that came from somewhere.

In another video posted on Vimeo (Josephs, 2018b), Omari Anderson, a student who participated in this project, shared his pride in being able to make music for a professional film that people enjoyed. He acknowledged that this had been a powerful learning experience and something he didn't think he'd ever have the opportunity to do, leading him to believe that he can do much more than he'd previously imagined.

To learn about more place-based projects at High Tech High that were fueled by student inquiry, go to the project page at www.hightechhigh.org/student-work/student-projects.

Science and Math Institute: Tacoma, Washington

Jutting into the south end of Puget Sound on the north end of Tacoma is Point Defiance Park, which is home to the Point Defiance Zoo and Aquarium. Deep within the more than 700-acre park is the Science and Math Institute (SAMi), a high school whose classrooms and labs provide space for classes in biotechnology, neuroscience, humanities, computer programming, music, and math. Students also use the park as a classroom in many locations. Up the trail at the Fort Nisqually Living History Museum site (originally a Hudson's Bay Company fort), students learn Washington state history. Over a mile away is SAMi's newest building, a joint-use space called the Environmental Learning Center, which houses labs, design spaces, discourse spaces, a makerspace, and an early learning center.

SAMi students learn by doing. For example, instead of sitting in a classroom and reading a textbook to learn about ethnobotany, they go out on the trails and sketch native plant species. After school, they serve as docents, and many hold internships at the zoo.

Exemplifying an inquiry-based approach to learning, Kennedy, a SAMi alum who is now a student at Howard University, decided to start a study group within the school and her greater community around the topic of "America Through the Lens of Blackness." She developed her senior project by coteaching a class on the same topic with a humanities teacher. Kennedy's goal was to intentionally explore narratives not brought forward in the dominant culture, and she succeeded beyond her initial vision. Her class, the first of many cotaught by students and staff, cleared a more authentic path for student voice and led to an accredited Comparative Cultures class at SAMi. It also helped her earn admission to Howard. In addition to enriching her school community, her experience helped her decide that whatever else she does, she will be a social justice advocate in her community and the larger world. As she puts it, "SAMi helped me run with my passions" (Vander Ark, 2016).

 ## Take Action

As teachers, we can take action toward building more inquiry-based learning environments. The following are steps you might consider and examples of the Inquiry-Based design principle as implemented by schools across the United States:

- ☐ **Incorporate big data and data analysis sprints.** Challenge students to ask questions around big-data sets. Have them dig deep to analyze data around complex topics using resources such as the search engine Wolfram Alpha; data tools developed by the nonprofit organization Gapminder; and the database and website Chronicling America, which provides access to historic newspaper articles. Students can use tools such as Data USA to analyze and investigate megatrends, cities, population growth, and other place-based topics of interest throughout their inquiry process.

☐ **Take a walk.** Especially with younger students, guide them along a sidewalk or take them to a park or other open space and provide quiet time for them to make observations and ask questions.

☐ **Use survey tools.** Jim Bentley, a National Geographic Fellow and current practicing teacher, uses tools such as Survey123 to engage students in inquiring about different places near and far. He encourages students to use tools that might not be designed specifically for K–12 classrooms but that they might use in the real world. For example, there are apps that help students gather, analyze, and understand their data in order to make the best decisions.

☐ **Set up question walls.** Designate a space in your learning area or classroom for posting student- and teacher-generated questions that emerge throughout the year. These questions can be the inspiration for future inquiry.

☐ **Use classroom openers.** Begin each day with a photo, video, or object and have students ask related questions. Repeated practice develops the ability to ask powerful questions that can begin an inquiry.

☐ **Assign mini research projects.** After students understand and know how to use inquiry tools, have them carry out an individual, original research project. Even young students can ask questions and collect data that are relevant. By owning the project from start to finish, students build agency around the inquiry process.

☐ **Engage students in phenology.** Phenology relates to the influence of climate on such annual phenomena as plant budding, animal migrations, and climate cycles. Have students track observations of the natural (and possibly human-built) world around them. They can create a monthly tracker on the wall to report their observations by day, week, month, or season. For example, they can report on birds observed, weather patterns, leaf color, moon cycle, or other natural phenomena. Helping students become more observant helps them become better at inquiry.

☐ **Ask students to share questions they have about their community.** High-quality projects and student work are often driven by a question that they generate.

☐ **Participate in interdisciplinary educator experiences.** Organizations such as the Wellborn Hub, the ECO Institute at the North Branch Nature Center in Vermont, the Teacher Learning Center at Teton Science Schools in Wyoming, and the Center for Place-Based Education at Antioch University New England offer place-based experiences for educators, helping them develop their understanding of the inquiry process. For example, as described on its website (https://northbranchnaturecenter.org/eco-institute), the ECO Institute "provides week-long, nature immersion courses for teachers, assistants, and administrators. The Institute is inquiry-based, outdoor learning through intensive experiential lessons, activities, and discussions" (ECO Institute, n.d.).

Learning Sciences Connection

The study of how people learn, more formally named "learning sciences," provides us with research that supports the place-based design principle and ideas discussed in this chapter. For more information, read *Designing for Learning* (Charlot et al., 2018). See also Figures 0.4 and 0.5 (pp. 7–8) in the Introduction. The Inquiry-Based design principle aligns with the following learning science principles:

- Cognition: 3
- Motivation: 7, 9
- Identity: 12
- Individual Variability: 14

5
Local to Global

With the end of empire, we are coming to an end of the epoch of rights. We have entered the epoch of responsibilities, which requires new, more socially-minded human beings and new, more participatory and place-based concepts of citizenship and democracy.

—**Grace Lee Boggs,** American author, activist, and philosopher

"Every country has beauty, every culture has beauty, and the more you know about the world, the easier it will be for you to succeed in it," says Jodiana Lombardi, a recent graduate of the Metropolitan Regional Career and Technical Center (MET) in Providence, Rhode Island. The MET is a pioneer school in the Big Picture Learning network (Hill, 2017). Schools in the Big Picture Learning network focus on place and leaving traditional four-walled school settings to learn. Elliot Washor, cofounder with Dennis "Doc" Littky of Big Picture Learning, shared in an interview, "You connect students to themselves by connecting them to places, adults, tools, and language out in the world."

Jodiana spent most of her time at the MET working on deep, meaningful place-based projects focused on refugee crises both local and global. As she explains, her curiosities about the world near and far started early:

When I was in second grade, we had an after-school program called "Passports from Around the World." We'd pretend we were on an airplane and then we'd be in a different country. The first country we ever learned about was Morocco, and I immediately fell in love with the history. I went home and told my mom I wanted to live there one day.

As I got older, my interest in North Africa spread to the Middle East and I fell in love with the culture. It's so rich and there's so much we aren't really exposed to outside of the war and the issues we have. I wanted the full story. (Hill, 2017, para. 5 and 6)

At the MET, Jodiana was immediately connected to a mentor who understood her passion for culture and the refugee population. Each project students work on at the MET requires that they connect their work to an issue or opportunity in their immediate community, so her mentor engaged her in an exploration of local refugee populations in Providence.

Jodiana learned that there was a booming population of refugees migrating to her hometown from Iran and other Middle Eastern countries. She found immediate opportunities to work directly with the local refugee population and eventually was able to make connections to groups overseas. While at the MET, Jodiana made two trips to the Middle East and returned each time with a deeper understanding of, and ability to better serve, her local community.

What Jodiana experienced was a powerful place-based project that connected her to both her local and global communities.

> "It's true, we are raising kids who need to know how they fit into a super-connected, global society. But our young people also need to learn how their decisions and actions impact the areas where they live.
> By becoming inquisitive, informed members of their own communities, students develop deeper connections with their place on earth, something they can then extend to other places. Educating for a better, more sustainable future needs to start at home."
>
> **—Sarah Anderson,**
> 2018, para. 15

The Principle: Local to Global

Young people want to tackle big challenges and local issues connected to global crises of our time. Big issues and opportunities—such as those related to dignity, equity, creating sustainable cities and habitats, eradicating poverty, developing more affordable and clean energy solutions—are increasingly pressing and challenging. We need a society equipped and dedicated to bettering our world and local communities.

Many global issues are also present in a local context. What makes something real and important is the local instantiation of the problem. It is the local experience that grounds students in an understanding of why something is important or why they might want to care. Unless they can connect to a tangible local version of something, it is hard for them to feel motivated enough to care. Connected learning experiences—experiences tied to real-world places or projects that students have a personal investment in—increase engagement, agency, and academic outcomes (Parsons & Taylor, 2011).

Some students may feel that they can't make a global impact, but we want them to understand that everyone can make a difference locally. We want them to realize that when we collectively attack a local challenge or opportunity, we are addressing some of these issues as part of a world community. When students start locally on a topic or issue of interest, they develop agency and compassion for that cause. When we then facilitate connections for them to a similar issue on a global scale, they come to realize that they have real potential to make an impact. Julie Keane (2016) states, "Local investigations put students in the driver seat. Local investigations provide compelling foundations for connecting student curiosity to global contexts because students can't begin to explore the world unless they recognize where they are."

Classrooms where students are engaging in local and global place-based investigations give educators an opportunity to be culturally inclusive. Culturally responsive classrooms are designed around who students are as individuals and what cultural assets they bring to a classroom. With increasingly diverse classrooms and dynamic cultures, it is unrealistic and ill-informed to assume a teacher can be the gatekeeper of cultural knowledge. Rather, local and global investigations tied to place allow for many cultures to be included and explored as a part of integrated learning experiences.

Local investigations allow students to discover and act upon issues of significance even if they cannot travel to another place for global learning. The inability of some students to travel because of financial, cultural, or other reasons can create inequities in a classroom; conducting local investigations or using tools to connect globally can help remedy this situation.

Finally, investigations can also go both ways. Students can start with a global issue or cause, such as those identified by the United Nations in its Sustainable Development Goals blueprint, and work to identify a local related issue or project to tackle. They can collect data to answer questions arising in classrooms, schools, or the larger communities around them (Keane, 2016).

What Does Local to Global Look Like in Practice?

How would Jodiana, whom we introduced at the start of this chapter, view the world without having had the place-based experiences she took part in? Even if a student is able to have just one such experience, either in their immediate community or far outside their ZIP code, it can be transformative and fuel many weeks of learning.

So what does this design principle look like in practice? Generally speaking, students coconstruct meaningful projects that are fueled by real local issues they care about and that have a global connection. For example, when a housing development resulted in clear-cutting more than 10 acres of forest behind Mukilteo Elementary School north of Seattle, students were heartbroken. They banded together in an environmental leadership group and developed a plan to restore and enhance an overgrown and forgotten two-acre parcel of land adjacent to the playground. With help from school volunteers and community groups such as the Boy Scouts, they created an outdoor classroom with an amphitheater and trails with information stations.

As demonstrated by the students at Mukilteo, empathy is developed when we engage in thinking about the experience of others. The Mukilteo students came face to face with urbanization and the loss of green space. The local issue exposed the students to a global issue. They responded with a design project that made a significant contribution to their community and also came to understand that places around the world are facing similar situations.

As noted earlier, sometimes students encounter a global issue and then make connections to how they might ameliorate or garner interest in a similar local issue. In another example, students at Normal Park Museum Magnet School in Chattanooga, Tennessee, started a place-based project by exploring the following question: "What do we care about in our own communities and want to help contribute to?" As a result of their exploration, they revealed other regions around the world with similar challenges and emerging solutions. Although they didn't visit every place they researched, their understandings were deeper and more robust because of the comparisons and considerations that emerged as a result of thinking about their own context and community (Knowles, 2019).

STAR School, located on the edge of the Navajo reservation outside Flagstaff, Arizona, was founded on the idea that "integration of culture and academics is not only a sound education practice, it's essential to the future success of the school's students" (STAR School's Story, 2016). STAR stands for Service to All Relations. Students at STAR work off the grid (the school generates its own electricity and grows its own food) on meaningful place-based projects tied to Navajo culture, beliefs, and practices, including care for the environment—a global concern. A recent project addressed issues related to the lack of available clean drinking water. Based on this need, students and the school staff developed a "water bus" that provides mobile, solar-powered water filtration for families in the region. The local need for clean potable water connected students to a worldwide issue.

How Technology Enhances Local Investigations and Global Connections

Students such as Jodiana are fortunate to have the opportunity to travel globally, but not all students can have first-hand experience in global settings—or even local ones, for that matter. Fortunately, an increasing number of online tools and opportunities are available to educators and students to engage them in places they otherwise might be unable to visit.

Even with just a basic smartphone, teachers and students can take part in a videoconference, record a video or audio clip, or look up relevant information. E-mail exchanges that enable students to learn from students in another place, with a different perspective—as basic as it sounds—are often transformative and can inform a better understanding of place. Technology can also allow for more frequent visits and conversations with experts, business partners, or community leaders with whom a student is working. Although not every school has the latest technology and digital tools available, access to the internet is expanding across the United States, and even if used just periodically during a place-based project or learning experience, online connections have incredible potential to engage students and enhance their learning.

As mentioned in Chapter 1, experiences that take place through mixed reality (including virtual and augmented reality) can enhance place-based learning. Of course, this technology has its limits. It provides only a fishbowl view of much broader contexts, and it doesn't allow for full, multisensory experiences. However, its use has many positive implications, especially when actual travel to a place is not possible.

 # Cases

The following examples illustrate how the Local to Global principle has been implemented in schools across the United States.

Oso New Tech High School: El Paso, Texas

Twenty yards from the U.S.-Mexico border, Jorge (a pseudonym) sits in a history and English class, working on a project about the border crisis and crime in Juárez, Mexico, the town across the Rio Grande from El Paso. Before attending Oso New Tech, Jorge thought his most viable option for the future was to go straight into the military, even if it meant dropping out and just getting a GED. He would then at least be able to see the world. He had always been curious about other places and passionate about finding a career that tied him to bigger issues than what he experienced in El Paso.

Oso New Tech is part of the New Tech Network, a nonprofit organization working to transform schools across the United States. The approach to teaching and learning is integrated, usually combining two or more subject areas. A growing number of New Tech Network schools in El Paso are seeing significant academic improvements, as well as positive social and emotional outcomes (EPISD and New Tech Network, 2018).

Upon arriving at Oso, Jorge quickly realized that El Paso had more to offer than he had previously thought. He learned through some of his initial projects that El Paso has an incredibly connected global market and economy that could offer him opportunities he had never believed were possible.

Mauricio Olague, a long-time El Paso resident and veteran art teacher at Oso, had a similar experience—though from an adult's perspective. After teaching for years in a traditional school environment, he felt burnt out, disconnected, and stagnant in terms of his personal and professional growth. Once he began teaching at Oso, however, he was able to incorporate what he knew and loved about his community into lessons and projects for students, and he could continue to learn about connections between the local economies, historical events, cultural resources, and places abroad.

With Mr. Olague's guidance, Jorge and his classmates learned about the murals around El Paso and their cultural and historical underpinnings. They studied the Dada art movement and engaged in provocative conversations. They were able to connect their art projects to what is going on in the world and nationally.

In another example of place-based work at Oso, social studies teacher Joel Rodriguez worked with his students to research nearby Presidio County and found out that it has small oil and gas deposits. Students knew there was a potential for fracking with the discovery of oil; therefore, they created a presentation about the pros and cons of the issue to their community.

Mr. Rodriguez and his students also investigated recycling in their community and presented their research findings to El Paso city representatives, pointing out that the downtown had no recycling bins. They shared research that highlighted how other cities across the nation deal with recycling issues and then put together a campaign to highlight better recycling practices. Students also held arts and crafts workshops that featured recyclable products and organized a massive cleanup at a local park as a companion piece to their "2,000 Bottles Plastic Recycling Campaign."

Teton Science Schools: Jackson, Wyoming, and Victor, Idaho

Teton Science Schools operates a PreK–12 school in Jackson, Wyoming, and a PreK–8 school in Victor, Idaho—both with place-based education deeply embedded in their missions. The Local to Global principle is evident in many place-based experiences as students connect local challenges with global challenges.

In a collaboration with Place Network Online, middle school students researched the concept of imports and exports in their community. They visited local businesses that exported goods and used imported materials. In the final component of the project, each student or group of students had to create an original product specifically marketed to a region of the world that appeared to have a need for such a product. Students came to understand how local microeconomies connect with the flow of goods and materials around the world. The project required systems thinking as well as a core focus on the Local to Global place-based education principle.

The 2019 U.S. government shutdown inspired elementary school students to launch a place-based investigation into food scarcity when they discovered that subsidy checks were not arriving for high-need families in the area. Students visited various food banks, investigated the costs of meeting basic food needs, and eventually created pottery for an "Empty Bowls" community fundraiser. Local supermarkets and restaurants donated food, and the proceeds from the event were donated back to local food-support agencies. Learning about the local need connected students to the global challenge of providing sufficient food for all people.

Albemarle County Public Schools: Charlottesville, Virginia

Learning in many Albemarle County classrooms is connected to place, particularly to the city of Charlottesville, Virginia. One example comes from Western High School, where cohorts of students work on integrated, place-based projects. (Much of this section is drawn from the results of our case study with this school [Getting Smart, 2018b].)

Ms. McLaughlin, a veteran teacher at Western, realized it became important to focus on projects that have deeper meaning or, as she says, "have some real community impact, real authenticity, either within the school or even in the larger Charlottesville community" (p. 6).

The National Writing Project worked with Western and students in a class cotaught by Ms. McLaughlin and Ms. Laux as part of a year-long grant-focused initiative where students were asked to consider how we, as a society, memorialize stories, and what monuments are built and why. They named it the Let 'Em Shine Project. Students had the opportunity to choose a story—a local story that hasn't been told—that currently doesn't have a monument or any exhibit. This has given them the freedom and creativity to tell that story in a really public way. The goal was for student projects to end up as a part of the fabric of Charlottesville. The teachers explain,

> We provide the structure and a little bit of the scaffolding and the due dates, and then we also try to have check-ins. We try to have meetings with students either if they are working in a group or on their own. We use Socratic Seminars and different workshop styles. . . . Students obtain feedback from each other and also from outside experts and community members. . . . [Students and] educators in ACPS also rely on university professors . . . to provide feedback and assist with work-shops, ensuring that students receive expert feedback. (p. 7)

The goal is that students link their understandings to more global and historical issues. As part of the Let 'Em Shine project, Laux and McLaughlin realized that looking back on one's efforts is incredibly important work, and that students ought to consider the impact far beyond the project they do in their classroom this year. As they put it,

> We want students to have long-term effects. When they go see a monument or memorial or to a museum, they should continue

> to ask questions like, "What story is being told? What story isn't being told?" We want them to look around with a more critical eye, so that it's not only that they're going to create something at the end, but rather as they go forward in life, there's always that idea about uncovering the story. (p. 7)

 Take Action

As teachers, we can take action toward using the Local to Global design principle in our classrooms. The following are steps you might consider and examples of the Local to Global design principle as implemented by schools across the United States:

☐ **Build a Local to Global news wall.** Have students bring in national and international news articles and add them to a Local to Global wall where they can make concrete connections to local and regional phenomena. For example, they may discover that global steel prices affect compensation at a local steel factory or that the existence of recycling programs depends on global demand for recycled goods.

☐ **Create a digital community newspaper.** Using simple technology tools, build a local news blog run exclusively by students. To cover English language arts targets, require that each student write at least one article a year about the local community. Promote the newspaper to parents to encourage a local following.

☐ **Create a virtual reality experience.** Build a local tour of your community focused on the three aspects of the Place Triangle (see Figure 2.1, p. 23) and share it via technology such as the Google Cardboard device. Find other schools across the globe to share with.

☐ **Connect to a global opportunity.** List global problems worth solving or refer to the UN's 17 Sustainable Development Goals. Have students link projects and tasks to these goals in a classroom display.

☐ **Build a learning community in your region.** Using an effort by LRNG, Chicago Cities of Learning, and Aurora Public Schools as an example, pilot a small, community-badging program that allows community organizations to post playlists, experiences, and challenges worth solving, and have students sign up and receive credit for completing these opportunities.

☐ **Connect virtually with another school.** Partner with another school to solve a common challenge (perhaps through the design thinking process described in Chapter 6).

☐ **Study exports and imports.** Have students investigate your community to determine inflows and outflows and identify if the community is a net exporter or net importer. Challenge students to identify possibilities for local production and micro-manufacturing to connect to the larger economic system.

☐ **Try a project with a global-issue focus and make local connections.** An increasing number of project-based learning examples are available online, including some from PBLWorks, CraftEd Curriculum, and EL Education. See, for example, the Think Globally, Act Locally example from PBLWorks and adapt materials and instruction as needed.

☐ **Connect globally to gain intercultural understandings.** Schools across the United States and around the world are connecting with one another to deepen intercultural understandings and levels of students' global competence, using tools such as Skype and Empatico (Lindsay, 2017). Connecting to collaborate on projects, share perspectives on similar topics, or just to have social exchanges is a great way to begin local-to-global place-based work in your classroom.

Learning Sciences Connection

The study of how people learn, more formally named "learning sciences," provides us with research that supports the place-based design principle and ideas discussed in this chapter. For more information, read *Designing for Learning* (Charlot et al., 2018). See also Figures 0.4 and 0.5 (pp. 7–8) in the Introduction. The Local to Global design principle aligns with the following learning science principles:

- Cognition: 3, 4
- Motivation: 7
- Identity: 12, 13
- Individual variability: 14

6

Design Thinking

Students shouldn't have to leave their community to live, learn, and earn in a better one.

—**Stephen Ritz,** educator and author

For more than a century, Grand Rapids, Michigan, has been known for design and manufacturing—especially of furniture. A secondary school that opened in 2015 is extending that design tradition. The Grand Rapids Public Museum School is located in a downtown museum site straddling the Grand River. The school was formed as a collaboration between the school district, the Grand Rapids Public Museum, the city, nonprofit partners, and two universities.

Principal Christopher Hanks describes the school's three core principles as follows:

> First, the museum is not just a set of artifacts, but a mindset and distillation of the entire community and region. Second, place-based education is a commitment to the community and the real-world learning assets it holds. And, third, design thinking is used as a method and set of processes for engaging students in learning and problem solving. (XQ, 2017, p. 2)

Projects, including one designed to become the largest river restoration project in the United States, takes students into every aspect of their community and its surrounding environment. "Our aim is engaged and empowered citizens," says Hanks. "What drives us is cultivating [the required] skills."

The museum is a resource students use nearly every day, but students also spend time working with community partners and collaborators all over the city, from universities and nonprofit groups to local scientists, artists, and business people. "We want to transform the students from consumers of education to producers of it," said Hanks (Vander Ark, 2018f, para. 3). "We're also interested in sustainability, about nature in the city, about being urban dwellers," added Hanks.

Designing for a place or a context helps build a more democratic society or helps those engaged to build a better existing community. Students feel like their work is usable, feasible, viable, and beneficial if they go through a full design thinking process. It also creates more ownership over their ability to create a solution and feel a part of the work. As Greg Smith, emeritus professor of education at Lewis and Clark College, said, "Students living in small towns or in big cities with lots of challenges are often encouraged to escape and seek opportunities elsewhere. Place-based education encourages students to envision what is possible and rather than escape, identify and design ways to make communities better" (Getting Smart, 2019).

 ## The Principle: Design Thinking

It is often stated at graduation ceremonies that this graduating class will change the world. This group is ready. Go forth and make a difference—*ad infinitum.* Given this, and the needs of the world, one would expect schools to be full of repeated practice in "solution finding" or "difference making."

But how often do young people play an active role in the community? How often do we as teachers allow students to engage with real opportunities to make a difference, with the students responsible for exploring, defining, testing, and refining possible solutions? Why do we expect students, after experiencing a teacher-directed, knowledge-based curriculum for 13 years (or more), to suddenly have the skills and dispositions to make innovative solutions and social change possible?

Schools that engage students in design thinking are seeing that students are ready to build solutions, create innovation, and make a difference—not just when they graduate, but now. The typical design thinking process includes several steps, all focused on creative problem solving that is rooted in empathy for a cause, an issue, or a group of people.

Place-based education prioritizes design thinking as a systematic process to design innovative solutions to challenging opportunities. To build community and support a thriving democracy, it is not enough to passively observe. Students must learn how to create and innovate around novel and complex challenges. Whereas experts have defined large-scale challenges such as the United Nations Sustainable Development Goals, design thinking embedded in place-based education allows students to grasp and address challenges on a local level. Figure 6.1 illustrates some of the new and complex benefits and challenges that have arisen in the last 10 years and are likely to be faced in the next 10 years.

Our world will become increasingly divided and inequitable if we don't look at a broad range of technologies for sharing the benefits and wealth created by exponential technology. Working together on place-based projects that use design thinking will bring us closer to solutions and to mitigating those potential equity gaps that new opportunities can create.

With the popularization of design thinking over the last 10 years through the work of the Stanford d.school and IDEO, among others, significant resources are now available for all teachers and students to more readily engage in design work (IDEO, n.d.; Stanford d.school, n.d.). The Teton Science Schools process (see Figure 6.2) is one example. The Engineering Practices articulated in the Next Generation Science Standards (n.d.) also provide tools and models around design engineering. All of these models illustrate the same concept—by building structures around the elusive nature of innovation, students can more readily innovate in the future.

FIGURE 6.1. **Benefits and Challenges of the Last 10 Years and the Next 10 Years**

Last 10 Years	Next 10 Years
Polarized politics	Increasing job dislocation
Social media violates privacy	3+ versions of web for privacy/censorship
Cameras and sensors everywhere	Expanded rideshare, autonomous vehicles
Artificial intelligence (AI) everywhere	Black box and bias problems with AI use
1+ billion lifted out of poverty	Growing income inequality
Cryptocurrency	Distributed ledgers track everything
Warming Earth, violent storms	Some climate solutions, some devastation

FIGURE 6.2. **Teton Science Schools Design Thinking Process**

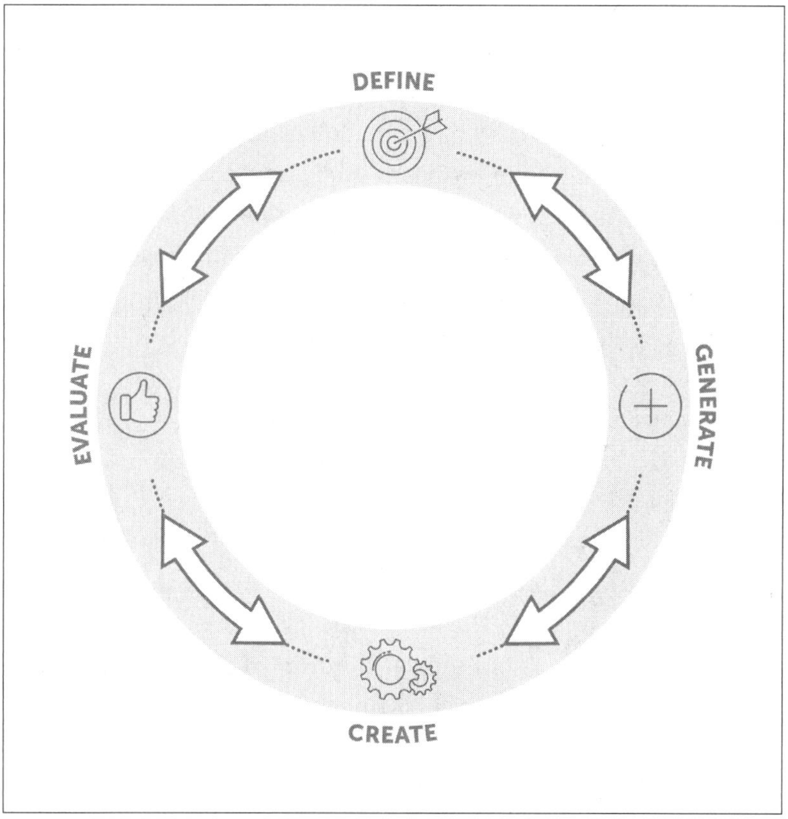

DEFINE
GENERATE
CREATE
EVALUATE

Source: Used with permission from Teton Science Schools, Jackson, WY.

When we guide students through the design thinking process, they eventually build ownership and agency to replicate the process without our support. This ability to replicate is critical to sustain local, regional, and global places. As shown in the Teton Science Schools model in Figure 6.2, the process is not circular but begins with the Define phase—defining the challenge. Students use tools such as the d.school's empathy map and the Designing for Equity self-reflection step to clearly see community needs—and their own biases in the process. Although typical design thinking processes consider only human need, place-based education expands this to include all components of the community, human or nonhuman.

Once the opportunity to innovate is defined, constraints are articulated to provide requirements on the solution. These constraints might be resource-based (not enough materials) or know-how-based (a lack of skills). In the Generate phase, multiple ideas are generated around the opportunity in ways that do not suppress out-of-the-box ideas. Individual brainstorming, sticky note "sort-and-clump" activities, and user stories can help generate more possible solutions. As a group settles on a first possible solution, they build a prototype during the Create phase to test with potential users. During prototype building, it is important to build a product or concept with minimum viability in order to get feedback quickly during the Evaluate phase. Each step in the process can be accessed from any other step—the concept of design thinking is nonlinear.

During the Evaluate phase, students should reflect on how the potential user experiences the solution and also reflect around constraints, using an innovation review tool such as the one shown in Figure 6.3. As students become more familiar with the evaluation tool, initial prototypes will become stronger. Equity in terms of the effect the proposed solution will have is thus increased by reflecting not only at the start of design but also at the end around whether the solution is good for people, place, and planet.

Like different levels of inquiry (see Chapter 1), different levels of design thinking can be implemented within the learner experience, as shown in Figure 6.4. Levels of learner responsibility increase as students repeatedly experience design thinking. Teachers can vary the type of design thinking they use based on the experience, development, and interests of students, as well as the teachers' comfort level.

The design thinking process requires students to consider novel and complex challenges and opportunities in their own backyards, and it prepares them for active community engagement. Design thinking in the context of place-based education presents them with arguably the most authentic and relevant challenges and opportunities for learning.

FIGURE 6.3. **Evaluating for Innovation**

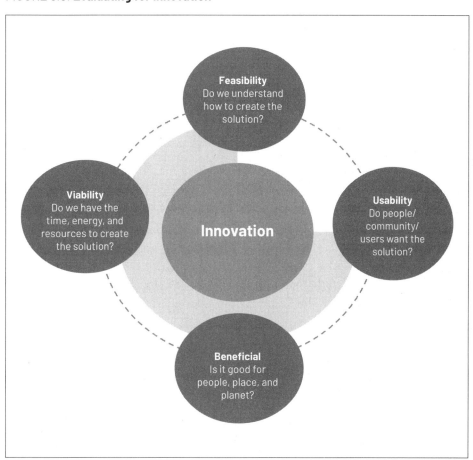

Source: Used with permission from Teton Science Schools, Jackson, WY.

FIGURE 6.4. **Levels of Design Thinking**

Design Level	Problem/Challenge	Constraints	Solution	Example
1. Confirmation design	Teacher provided	Teacher provided	Teacher provided	Students are assigned to community service or service learning.
2. Structured design	Teacher provided	Teacher provided	Student generated	Teacher identifies a challenge and tells students to figure out how to fix it within predetermined constraints.
3. Guided design	Teacher provided	Student generated	Student generated	A teacher notices that the class is disruptive and has students find a solution to the problem within constraints they determine.
4. Open design	Student generated	Student generated	Student generated	Students go into the community to discover opportunities for design projects.

Source: Used with permission from Teton Science Schools, Jackson, WY.

 Cases

Schools around the world are adopting design thinking as their main approach to teaching and learning. The following are examples of such schools.

Normal Park Museum Magnet School: Chattanooga, Tennessee

Normal Park Museum Magnet School partners with seven local museums and centers to enhance each student's learning experience (Normal Park Museum Magnet School, n.d.). At least one day a week, students are off campus at one of the museums, working on integrated lessons and projects. Every several months, students lead parents, fellow students, and community members around their school to see exhibits that highlight projects they have worked on.

Grant Knowles, a teacher at Normal Park Museum Magnet School, realized several years ago that design thinking was going to provide his students with a deeper sense of commitment, agency, and purpose. He began by introducing students to the Empathy component of thinking by design and encouraging them to imagine products they could create that might address a real-world need or cause. This combination of design thinking and place-based experiences has been transformative for his teaching and for his students' learning. The community already was his students' classroom, but now they were able to imagine what they might actually do to improve their community.

"Students will dive into social and local issues, especially those students who might not seem to be as engaged and interested normally," Grant said. "I used to think that providing some students with more challenging tasks was out of their reach, when, in fact, it was exactly what they needed—a push and to be passionate about what they were working on."

In one example, what started as a *Shark Tank*–style design challenge around social issues turned into a three-year effort by three black students. Empathizing with other people of the black community in Chattanooga, they decided to try to tackle world racism. They quickly found that there were issues locally—in fact, right in their own school—that they could address through design thinking and a focus on place.

They realized that collectively, the three of them—not yet finished with 6th grade—had attended 11 schools. At each school, they had experienced some form of segregation, including students self-segregating—especially in the lunchroom, where teachers weren't available to help form meaningful groups and relationships. Their project idea, after several iterations, was to create table-top solutions (creative conversation starters) to rotate people throughout the cafeteria, providing more opportunities for students to learn about one another.

Design39Campus: Poway, California

North of San Diego, Design39Campus, a K–8 school in the Poway Unified School District, uses design thinking to engage students in interdisciplinary place-based work. The school itself was designed and built for place-based work, with nooks, corners, and open spaces that allow students to engage in design thinking projects.

For example, kindergarteners learned about homes around the world (Pujar, 2016). They unpacked local home structures (i.e., they learned about different home styles and ways of living), and they read about different places and home styles. They then created their own "dream homes" by coming up with floor plans and designs that tapped into mathematical understandings and skills.

University Charter School: Livingston, Alabama

University Charter School is housed at the University of West Alabama, located near the Alabama-Mississippi border in a rural area that struggles with pervasive poverty. As part of its mission (and as a partner with the Place Network), the school uses place-based education as a means to reimagine the region and to support a generation of students who not only understand the challenges but also come up with solutions to increase long-term community sustainability. In an effort to understand local agriculture, students are designing a school garden, chicken coop, and composting system for the campus. Using design thinking principles, they are generating different ideas for each individual component, prototyping and evaluating the solutions, and planning for construction of the full system. As part of the place-based curriculum, this project not only serves to help students learn about local ecology and economics but also supports the development of students as project managers and solution makers.

Take Action

As teachers, we can take action toward using design thinking in place-based environments. The following are steps you might consider and examples of design thinking as implemented by schools across the United States:

- ☐ **Conduct community opportunity surveys.** Survey parents and community members to identify real needs in the community. Have students review and select challenges to address through place-based projects.

- ☐ **Rethink the classroom.** Introduce design thinking methodology to redesign the classroom learning space (walls, furniture, etc.).

- ☐ **Create mini makerspaces.** Create a mini makerspace in your classroom that allows students to build and make things using simple supplies.

- ☐ **Present design challenges.** Present weekly or monthly design challenges for students to complete independently.

- ☐ **Embed the design thinking process in decision making.** Build anchor charts for the classroom around design thinking so that it becomes a common problem-solving tool (see IDEO, www.ideo.com, or d.school, https://dschool.stanford.edu, for tool collections).

- ☐ **Have students generate challenges worth solving.** Create a space in the classroom where students can post challenges of interest to them.

- ☐ **Support a student-run business.** At One Stone, a high school in Boise, Idaho, students run a marketing and design firm called Two Birds, interacting with adults at all levels of the business. Students take adults through the design thinking process and use it in their own work. Throughout the process they consider context and place as key factors for whatever they design and create for their clients. Many schools across the United States are partnering with Real World Scholars and, through their EdCorps program, are empowering students to create their own businesses.

- ☐ **Connect with industry to create.** At e3 Civic High in San Diego and Vista Innovation and Design Academy in Vista, California, students use the design thinking process, especially focusing on the element of empathy, to cocreate meaningful place-based projects with industry partners (Liebtag, 2017c). Partners include local libraries, large technology corporations, and hospitals, all of which have human-centered design challenges that they want students to help them tackle. Students at e3 work over the course of six months on projects to "engage, educate and empower scholars to solve personalized complex problems that positively impact local and/or global communities" (e3 Civic High, n.d., para. 1).

Learning Sciences Connection

The study of how people learn, more formally named "learning sciences," provides us with research that supports the place-based design principle and ideas discussed in this chapter. For more information, read *Designing for Learning* (Charlot et al., 2018). See also Figures 0.4 and 0.5 (pp. 7–8) in the Introduction. The Design Thinking principle aligns with the following learning science principles:

- Cognition: 4, 5
- Motivation: 7, 9, 10
- Identity: 12
- Individual Variability: 14

7

Interdisciplinary

Successful instruction is constant, rigorous, integrated across disciplines, connected to students' lived cultures, connected to their intellectual legacies, engaging, and designed for problem solving that is useful beyond the classroom.

—**Lisa Delpit,** *"Multiplication Is for White People":*
Raising Expectations for Other People's Children

Kesia grew up on the South Side of Chicago, still lives there, and has no plans to leave anytime soon. However, this wasn't always the case. Her experiences throughout middle school led her to believe that she didn't have a place in the world.

She'd experienced real life outside school and realized that what she was learning had no connection to who she was or where she came from. She learned math in isolation, literacy in isolation, and didn't see the connection between subjects. But in the real world, she had a wealth of experiences that were interconnected and formative.

It wasn't until she found herself at Chicago Tech Academy that she realized how the interconnectedness of the real world could also be valuable in her formal schooling. Chicago Tech Academy is "an educational community whose mission is to educate, empower, and connect a diverse next generation of entrepreneurial thinkers to discover their passions, succeed in college, and thrive in a digital world" (Chicago Tech Academy, n.d., para. 1).

Chicago Tech believes in

- Project-based learning to encourage a deeper, connected form of evidence-based education.
- An integrated college preparatory curriculum that fosters critical thinking and intellectual curiosity.
- Creating and sustaining a collaborative teaching and learning environment that explores and refines the ways students learn best.
- Helping students to become leaders and lifelong learners, through partnerships with the Chicago tech community.
- Encouraging students to develop meaningful relationships with peers, faculty and the business community through networking and internship opportunities.
- Graduating entrepreneurial-minded, fearless, confident and connected learners who take responsibility for their lives and give back to the community. (Chicago Tech Academy, n.d., para. 1)

At Chicago Tech Academy and through the Embarc Chicago program, which is focused on rich place-based experiences (Embarc Chicago, n.d.), Kesia worked on community-driven projects that have propelled her to become an advocate for other schools and resulted in students having richer learning experiences. Kesia reflected on her experience with Embarc:

I was a part of Embarc since my freshman year, starting with leadership academy (which was amazing). Being a part of Embarc has molded me into the courageous leader I am today. I was able to be a part of an expedition to Greenland . . . where I was pushed to what I used to consider my limits emotionally and physically. I then learned through tons of conversations with indigenous people, many thought-producing activities, and many instances of feeling like I failed. (personal communication, 2019)

 ## The Principle: Interdisciplinary

The world is interdisciplinary, but classrooms or sections of classroom time are traditionally isolated in subject areas. Math happens at this time, science next, and so on. This structure has clear benefits for teaching core skills of literacy and mathematics. However, when we consider the complexity of the world—whether human-designed or natural—it is easy to see the interconnectedness of content and ideas. Interdisciplinary approaches are not new and are commonly used in constructivist environments (Science Education Research Center, n.d.).

The idea that you could teach about the ocean in science without embedding literacy skills at some point is hard to imagine. Although the overlap of most core content areas is readily apparent to many educators, many are not encouraged to explore these intersections and teach in an interdisciplinary way. Yet the personal and professional lives of most adults are interdisciplinary. Most decisions and projects require content and skills from various disciplines.

David Sobel of Antioch University shares how place-based education is interdisciplinary: "Place-based education is the process of using the local community and environment as a starting point to teach concepts in language arts, mathematics, social studies, science, and other concepts across the curriculum" (2005, p. 6).

Place can be used not only as a starting point but also as a connector to bring coherence to a disconnected curriculum as students prepare for the world beyond school. Various researchers have articulated the difference between *interdisciplinary* and *transdisciplinary* approaches, with *inter* implying that disciplines exist and *trans* articulating an approach in which discipline does not exist (Jeder, 2014). This completes the articulation of approaches starting with *intra, cross, multi, inter,* and *trans* (Stember, 1991). Also, much has been written on concept-based curriculum as a clear approach to integrate content and skills around integrating concepts (Erickson, 2007).

How can place-based education support learning experiences that are interdisciplinary? How can agency, equity, and community be supported through these approaches? As we explore the interdisciplinary nature of place-based education in this chapter, we link the principle to agency, equity, and community. Project-based learning is a key tool for building agency through place-based projects. Interdisciplinary approaches can increase equity as students explore perspectives from multiple content areas. Finally, communities are inherently interdisciplinary—and students can increase their impact on their community when they see its interdisciplinary nature.

Building Agency Through Project-Based Learning

As noted, place-based education often is interdisciplinary and project-based. Again, although it doesn't have to have these characteristics, when it does, the result is usually deeper learning and more meaningful work for students

(Smith, 2016). Students build agency as they implement projects that are relevant, meaningful, and impactful.

The tools of project-based learning are well documented through the PBLWorks group (formerly the Buck Institute; www.pblworks.org) and the High Quality PBL website (https://hqpbl.org). Key components include core driving questions, a focus on process, authentic assessment, and real-world connections. High-quality, project-based learning is strongest when it combines multiple subject areas (High Quality Project-Based Learning, n.d.).

Terms

Integrated: Incorporating at least two subject areas and requiring students to use skills or knowledge in those subject areas to tackle a problem, address a task, or complete an assignment.

Project-based learning: Learning in which students work on a project over an extended period of time—from a week to a semester—that engages them in solving a real-world problem or answering a complex question. They demonstrate their knowledge and skills by developing a public product or presentation for a real audience (PBLWorks, n.d.).

An example of a place-based experience that was also integrated and project-based involved middle school students at Mountain Academy of Teton Science Schools in Idaho, part of the Place Network. The students investigated bird ecology and roadside raptor mortality as a way to learn ecosystem impacts. The students' learning incorporated social studies, as they met with legislators to advocate for more road signs to alert drivers to the presence of raptors; and English, through letter-writing campaigns to build awareness of the issue in the community. The students also developed leadership skills as they coordinated a townwide road-cleanup day. Students were assessed in terms of the various learning goals required for each discipline.

Another example comes from Napa Junction, a project-based elementary school in American Canyon, California. "All of our units begin with Next Generation Science Standards so they are all STEM connected," said school principal Donna Drago (personal communication, February 26, 2019). Every field trip extends the learning of a unit. Drago shared two examples:

- Second graders visited Connolly Ranch to learn about farm life, the role of animals, ecology, sustainability, and an appreciation for nature. They worked in the garden, harvested vegetables, and prepared a healthy meal with the harvest.

- Fourth graders studying alternative energy sources took a field trip to the local high school, which is powered by solar and geothermal energy. Based on what they learned, they made recommendations to the architects designing their new school building.

Well-conceived project- and place-based learning should incorporate challenges that enable students to work toward their individual learning goals and to fully engage and contribute. The same is true for a team-based project. For example, 8th graders at Meadow Valley School in Idaho, part of the Place Network Schools, realized they needed to work together to support local families affected by a housing crisis in the area. They worked as a team to build an 8-by-24-foot tiny home. To prepare, they studied "housing in their region and around the world, green living, grant writing, the trades, construction, repurposing, and even . . . real estate sales" (Teton Science Schools, 2019). Ultimately, they built a house for a community member in need.

Too often, place-based experiences end up being field trips—isolated events or one-time adventures (planned or unplanned) that lead to short-term outcomes and brief inspirational effects instead of long-lasting learning. Of course, many field trips are incredibly powerful, well thought out, and integrated into existing curriculum; but we advocate for more consistent use of place. Place, coupled with longer-term, integrated projects, ultimately yields long-term learning and connection to community.

Building Equity Through Multiple Perspectives

Often, the lens of a single discipline restricts perspective and introduces bias that may decrease equity in teaching and learning. When we introduce an interdisciplinary approach and connect it to place, we introduce multiple perspectives and expose inherent biases.

For example, when students learn about genetics in science in a way that focuses only on the ability of the environment to shape genetic code over generations, they miss opportunities to increase relevance through the study of epigenetics and social science. A concurrent focus on adverse childhood experiences (ACEs) related to epigenetics can connect the topic to a challenging, lived experience for some students. Additionally, those who have not experienced ACEs can begin to understand the lives of others with whom they learn every day.

Design thinking and interdisciplinary principles can be combined to expose bias in learning experiences if we adopt the reflective practices suggested by Stanford's d.school before undertaking any design process (Stanford d.school, n.d.). In what is called "equity-centered design," students are asked to acknowledge any preconceived biases through a Notice phase before defining the challenge.

Additionally, perspectives from different disciplines can help inform our own biases. The concept of westward expansion, widely described in texts about the United States, can be put in the context of Native American genocide to provide multiple discussion points for biases that can inform any history of a local place.

Building Community in an Interdisciplinary World

The world is interdisciplinary. If students are to fully participate in their communities as adults—a foundational building block to a thriving and sustainable region or nation—then they must be exposed to multiple experiences that reflect the real world. Consider any town council or county commission meeting across the United States. These meetings almost always allow public comment, and typically the topic is complex; many citizens may feel uninformed or unprepared for comments beyond an emotional reaction. Adults need to be able to draw on expertise from the sciences, social studies, mathematics, and literacy to clearly articulate and argue points to support a better and stronger community. Complex issues around immigration, housing, transportation, and resource management introduce multiple discipline topics and ideas. Practice in digesting, synthesizing, and acting on these issues is critical for the K–12 learner.

Jim Bentley, a National Geographic educator from Sacramento, California, has taken an interdisciplinary place-based approach to his instruction. In one example, students analyzed the distribution of water in their community to better understand how to reduce plastic waste. "Middle school students don't want to be wasteful and are very aware of the negative impact they might be making by using too much plastic," Bentley noted (personal communication, February 10, 2019). Students surveyed local businesses and the schools looking for water stations to refill bottles. They found only six stations in the area of the school district and began working to improve the situation. To better understand how plastics in general get used and end up being ocean waste, they expanded the project by learning about the flow of plastics from suburb to sea.

Approaches such as those used by Bentley can build agency, equity, and community. Any classroom teacher can start small to incorporate the Interdisciplinary principle into his or her work—even in the most prescriptive of curricula—by using the action steps presented near the end of this chapter.

EL Education—Examples of Projects Tied to Place

In its own words, EL Education, a community of educators, was "born out of a collaboration between the Harvard Graduate School of Education and Outward Bound USA. What started as a concept has grown into a movement. Our mission, now as then, is to create classrooms where teachers can fulfill their highest aspirations and students achieve more than they think possible, becoming active contributors to building a better world" (EL Education, n.d.).

A growing network of EL Education schools around the world engages students in meaningful, integrated projects that are often place-based. Students embark on expeditions that are tied to their community or a real-world issue. Examples of these projects, including 18 that are labeled as Better World Projects, can be found on their Models of Excellence web pages (https://modelsofexcellence.eleducation.org).

 # Cases

The following examples illustrate how the Interdisciplinary principle is being implemented through place-based experiences in schools across the United States.

Eagle Rock School: Estes Park, Colorado

Jon Anderson, an educator for more than 20 years (most of which have been at Eagle Rock, located near Rocky Mountain National Park), acknowledges place-based education as the school's core component. One interdisciplinary project in particular stands out to him as being incredibly influential in students' lives. The Dragonfly Project started out in his classroom of about 12 students who noticed that the area's dragonfly population was dwindling and were curious about what was affecting the insects' reproduction. Students who had never been comfortable touching bugs ended up leading a world-class research project that tracked, analyzed, and communicated what was going on with the local larvae.

Students were asked to partner with the National Park Service to develop solutions for sustaining the dragonflies in the region and informing other parks about their project. Now in place in more than 60 parks nationwide, the Dragonfly Project has left, and will continue to leave, its mark on the nation's ecosystems.

Anderson realizes that not every student has Rocky Mountain National Park in his or her backyard, but he has worked with educators around the United States to figure out how they might develop interdisciplinary projects tied to their local contexts or settings. In a personal interview (September 2018), he said this:

> I think place-based education is an easy fit for me; it really allows for integration between all different subject areas (literacy and science, . . . social studies, etc.). It can be done in other places and in cities as well. It's naturally integrated and not a forced facilitation of [the] Interdisciplinary [principle].

He also shared his thoughts on how place-based education directly addresses inequities:

> Eagle Rock by design is hoping to address inequities students face in school across the U.S. We are a place focused on the learners. We are an intentionally diverse school, and so we've had to be sure the park has done a good job at increasing relevance for all students. We are super-intentional about conversations around diversity and equity. I'm a big white guy with a beard, so we talk about that. One of the pieces of our program since 2008 has been addressing diversity, and the Park Service saw

the need for it. We ask ourselves often, how does the park stay relevant? We designed curriculum around that for students. Outcomes of that have been letters to the park superintendent with recommendations, conversations with their leadership about diversity and including student perspectives, as well as the need to have materials in Spanish and other languages.

Student Vidal Carrillo shared his thoughts about the effect of these experiences: "If I hadn't gone to Eagle Rock and met Jon, I probably would have dropped out of high school. If I stayed in Los Angeles, I may or may not be in jail right now. I would be a completely different person" (Skenazy, 2018).

Lake Elementary School: Vista, California

Located just north of San Diego, Vista Unified School District has been working to transform what teaching and learning look like. Erik Ray, an educator at Lake Elementary School, is working to tap into student strengths and interests by engaging students in interdisciplinary place-based learning. He has found through place-based projects that not only are his students reengaged in their learning but also this way of teaching and learning has the power to reengage teachers in the profession. Ray shared the following example of a place-based project that engaged students by tapping into literacy, science, and mathematics skills and knowledge:

Driving Question: Why are pollinators so important, and how can we help pollinators that are disappearing in our local community?

Project Description: Students first identified the global problem of pollinator decline and how it is affecting the local community. Students launched their inquiry by engaging in fieldwork at Guajome Regional Park.

Students further developed their literacy skills through reading informational text, navigating text features, and researching to build knowledge about the local issue. Students studied the different types of pollinators and the plants they help pollinate. In particular, students learned how butterflies are crucial pollinators in our local ecosystem and are in decline. They analyzed the numbers and population decline to assess what was going on and how rapidly the change had occurred.

Essential questions (these were uncovered during field work):

- How do plants grow and survive?
- How do pollinators help plants grow and survive?
- How do we get the fruits and veggies we eat?
- Why should people help pollinators survive?
- How can I take action to help pollinators?

Products/Exhibition: After carrying out multiple investigations with plants and seeds in science labs, students used design thinking to build, test, and refine hand pollinators that could be used in our school garden. We then used a formalized brainstorm process to address the question "How can we take action to help pollinators?" With students' knowledge of opinion writing, we decided we could write opinion pieces making the case to protect pollinators in our local community. These opinion pieces went on the back of seed packets with detailed scientific drawings of butterflies. Students chose to put milkweed and marigold seeds in their packets after learning that butterflies need these plants to survive. Students then distributed these packets to our school and local community.

Energy Institute High School: Houston, Texas

Formed in partnership with many oil industry leaders, Energy Institute High is a project-based school that explores energy issues, both locally and globally, through interdisciplinary place-based projects. Jenna Moon, head of partnerships for the school, knew that students weren't going to be interested in predetermined projects that were focused on a single subject (Liebtag, 2018). She, along with the rest of the Energy team, found that true interdisciplinary exploration about what is going on in the world around students leads to more meaningful work (Liebtag, 2017b).

Designing Sustainable Cities was a cross-curricular project that incorporated environmental science, environmental engineering, U.S. history, and English. Students developed solutions that addressed sustainability concerns at the micro and macro level. They created a plan to develop a personal habit that supports a sustainable lifestyle. Teams of students worked with key stakeholders to develop a plan that would address a sustainability concern within the city of Houston and hosted an evening exhibition that educated visitors about how individuals and cities can live more sustainably.

Another example project had students exploring energy use on the Energy Institute High School campus. They began by conducting an energy audit of the campus that analyzed the school's energy consumption, including lights, vampire devices (devices that consume energy even when turned off), and phone-charging stations.

In their English class, students researched several different options for using solar power. In their world geography class, they looked at the use of solar panels in different countries. In biology, they researched how different types of cells create and store energy and compared photosynthesis to cellular respiration. In engineering classes, students designed and built solar-powered chargers that were eventually distributed to each classroom for students to use to charge cell phones on campus. One year after implementation, students conducted another energy audit on campus to compare energy use before and after the solar chargers were created.

Take Action

As teachers, we can take action toward building interdisciplinary projects and instruction. The following are steps you might consider and examples of the Interdisciplinary design principle from schools across the United States:

- ☐ **Build your first project.** Do you teach only one subject and find it difficult to envision how you might facilitate an interdisciplinary project? Start with a unit you have taught in the past or a previous lesson and try to identify how you could have students elaborate on a particular aspect by incorporating another discipline. Use tools like the CraftED PBL Planning Guide or the Project Planner from PBLWorks to get started.

- ☐ **Meld place-based learning into coplanning across disciplines.** Are you already working across disciplines or coteaching? Try to coplan a project in which standards and objectives traverse subject areas *and* engage students in some form of place-based learning.

- ☐ **Develop interdisciplinary driving questions.** Work with colleagues and students to craft driving questions that naturally lend themselves to multiple subject areas or disciplines. You can use existing driving questions as starting points.

- ☐ **Seek authentic partners and audiences.** Do an asset map of your immediate school and local communities. Who can students work with to enhance their work? Instead of relying on those who frequently volunteer or otherwise contribute, get creative in identifying potential allies. We have seen interdisciplinary place-based projects in which students worked with local stores, universities, nonprofits, and government agencies.

- ☐ **Visit another classroom.** In person or virtually, visit another classroom that is doing this work well. Schools featured in this book welcome invitations to learn together. You can also search #placebaseded on Twitter for possible connections. Learn from and with these educators about their interdisciplinary place-based learning environments.

- ☐ **Explore place-based postsecondary programs.** Programs such as CITYterm (www.cityterm.org) and Minerva (www.minerva.kgi.edu) offer students and adults place-based postsecondary learning experiences. Students who may not have had the opportunity to live and learn in a city or a rural part of the world can experience a different way of living, learn about varied cultures, and gain new networks and opportunities, all while learning multiple subject areas and content. Elizabeth Irvin, a high school student at the time, shared her thoughts about her place-based experience in New York City:

> I feel like my experience with place-based education prepared me to thrive in every aspect of my being, and in turn, has influenced my life post-CITYterm. By immersing myself fully in this style of learning, I was able to uncover new academic interests that I may hope to pursue as a career. (Irvin, 2018, para. 6)

Learning Sciences Connection

The study of how people learn, more formally named "learning sciences," provides us with research that supports the place-based design principle and ideas discussed in this chapter. For more information, read *Designing for Learning* (Charlot et al., 2018). See also Figures 0.4 and 0.5 (pp. 7–8) in the Introduction. The Interdisciplinary design principle aligns with the following learning science principles:

- Cognition: 2, 3, 4
- Motivation: 7
- Identity: 12
- Individual Variability: 14, 15, 16

8

A Place-Based Education How-to Guide

One of the greatest challenges with a new teaching model or approach is determining how and where to get started. In this chapter, you will find starting points and ideas for how to begin your place-based education journey. Keep in mind that you can use place-based education as your only approach or just one part of your instructional repertoire. If you have already begun your place-based journey, you'll also find helpful tips for how to enhance your practices and students' experiences.

As you build your place-based practices, remember that there is no one-size-fits-all model. Place-based education as an overall approach encompasses many different learning models and outcomes, with no detailed roadmap to implementation that will work in every context. In fact, place-based education is not new; it has been evolving as a formal approach to schooling for generations (for more on the historical underpinnings of place-based education, read "The Past, Present and Future of Place-Based Learning," by Gregory Smith [2016]). Regardless, it can build agency, equity, and community for your students.

This entire guide and the resources mentioned are downloadable on the place-based education microsite (www.gettingsmart.com/placebasededucation). The guide consists of the following components:

1. Can I Do PBE in My Setting?
2. A Review of Place-Based Education Principles
3. Place-Based Resources
4. Implementation
5. Barriers
6. Stakeholder Starting Points

Can I Do PBE in My Setting?

Place-based learning can truly happen anytime, anywhere—on a field trip or in cities, rural villages, parks, or your hometown, school, or backyard. Although this list is by no means exhaustive, it captures the range of possibilities. We believe that every place has rich opportunities to embed learning into the local place.

Urban Settings

- Supported by Global Learning Models, the GCE Lab School in Chicago leverages relationships with more than 200 partners to "make the entire city a fertile learning environment" through its City2Classroom program. Read more about the Global Learning Models in "Preparing #LifeReady Students: Creating Globally-Sourced, Locally-Relevant Curriculum" (Davis, Rae, & Leite, 2017).

- Metro Charter Elementary in rapidly developing downtown Los Angeles leverages neighborhood resources—parks, cultural centers, businesses, and historical sites—to provide meaningful learning opportunities and enhance the experiences for diverse students. Kids take public transit for field trips and visit places such as City Hall and Disney Concert Hall.

- Horace Mann Elementary School in Washington, D.C., has food gardens and university partnerships. The entryway includes a garden wall with art that spells out values evident in every classroom: adventure, discovery, inspiration, and imagination. (Listen to the podcast about their design principles: www.gettingsmart.com/2016/04/getting-smart-podcast-horace-mann -elementary-where-a-shared-pedagogy-vision-informs-design-principles.)

- The Tacoma School District in Washington state has three high schools that partner with community organizations: Tacoma School of the Arts, the Science and Math Institute, and the School of Industrial Design, Engineering and Art (IDEA). At all of these schools, students use community resources to explore their passions.

- In his article "Putting the City at the Heart of Place-Based Education," author Daniel Rabuzzi (2016) describes how "place" can be different cities or neighborhoods, street corners, ball courts, barber shops, bus stops, and parades. Nature, too, can play a role in urban places, he says, in the form of a community garden or a river winding through the city.

- An orchard was the result of a brainstorm by five middle school students in Kansas City, Kansas, about a change they wanted to see in their school and community. With the help of a local organization called the Giving Grove, this idea of providing healthy produce spread to five other area schools that joined in planting trees that are expected to yield 25,000 pounds of fruit annually.

Rural Settings

- The Rural Schools Collaborative believes in the power of partnerships and place-based education to strengthen the bond between school and community. The collaborative highlights a number of exemplary efforts on rural place-based learning and provides useful research and resources for educators and communities.

- Giving back to communities helps increase student motivation. Highland Community School District in rural southwestern Wisconsin revamped its structure and curriculum to focus on environmental place-based learning that supports community life. At Northern Waters Environmental School, for example, middle and high school students work with community partners to solve local challenges.

- Students learn on a barge at New Harmony High in Venice, Louisiana. Students explore their passions, their community, and the world with an emphasis on a key issue for the region: coastal restoration.

- The Place Network is a network of rural place-based schools sharing the same place-based model. It was founded by Teton Science Schools, which has a total of four campuses in Wyoming and Idaho.

- In an interview on the Getting Smart podcast, author Anna Luhrmann tells her story of loving place-based education in the natural world of Grand Teton National Park. When she had to leave to finish her studies, she found that the town of Laramie, Wyoming, had a lot to offer place-based learners. She adopted the motto "Every Place Is Special or No Place Is Special."

Museums and the Arts

- At the New York Hall of Science, students and families design, make, and play with technology and other tools and materials. One set of apps called Noticing Tools helps users notice the math and science around them and opportunities to reshape and remake the world.

- Local museums and theaters are some of the places that help students stay engaged and build civic pride at Capital Community College in Hartford, Connecticut. When students come out of the classroom, off the campus, and into the community, they can connect with their community in meaningful ways.

- The museum is the school at Michigan's Grand Rapids Public Museum School.

- E3 Civic High School is housed in the spectacular new San Diego library.

- Tacoma School of the Arts has active relationships with each of the museums in downtown Tacoma. Classes are taught at the Tacoma Art Museum and the LeMay Car Museum. Plans call for a full-time arts liaison to strengthen relationships between the city, the museums, and the school.

- Houston A+ UP was launched as a small pilot middle school and expanded into a small charter network in 2019. Every week, A+ UP students ride public transit to visit an amazing network of museum and community partners.

- Led by former assistant superintendent Donna Deeds, the Museum at Prairiefire in Overland Park, Kansas, partners with Kansas City schools to bring natural history to life. Listen to a podcast in which Deeds describes this regional place-based learning gem and CAPS, the work-based initiative she created before joining the museum (www. gettingsmart.com/2016/08/20-schools-and-networks-that-educate -with-a-sense-of-place).

City, State, and National Parks

- Science teacher Mike Mihalic has called national parks "America's Best Idea and America's Best Classroom." They can be an exciting place for students to learn science, and field trips to the parks often fuel a lasting connection to the outdoors. In their article "6 Reasons You Should Work in America's Parks and Forests," Bonnie Lathram and Andrew Frishman (2016) tout the benefits of working in national parks and forests. Their ideas range from learning "about self" to learning "under duress."

- A city park in Sea Tac, Washington, plays a central role in the Highline School District's Marine Science Technology program. Housed at the Puget Sound Skills Center in the park, students use the location to learn about marine science and related skills.
- Eagle Rock is a small high school in Estes Park, Colorado, that takes full advantage of its location near Rocky Mountain National Park.
- Teton Science Schools partners with Grand Teton National Park in Wyoming to offer a variety of place-based opportunities for students around the country, as well as through the schools they operate.

Colleges and Universities

- Students at Humboldt State University in California are using the nearby Klamath River as a focal point for a science program that goes beyond the lab. The aim of the Klamath Connection is to boost the success of science, technology, engineering, and math (STEM) majors by connecting science, communities, and cultural perspectives.
- As director of the Hartford Heritage Project at Capital Community College in Hartford, Connecticut, Jeffrey Partridge has spent time researching place-based education. One result of his work is "Resources and Quotes on the Power of Place," which is a portal to resources for others starting place-based education at the college level.
- Some higher education institutions are succeeding at making place-based education central to their identity. The article "Higher Ed Approaches to Empowering Students" by Jeffrey Partridge (2016) shares the stories of Guttman Community College in New York City, Temple University in Philadelphia, and Capital Community College in Hartford, Connecticut.

Early Education Settings

- The Seattle area has at least a dozen preschool programs with an outdoor focus. Preschoolers at Fiddleheads Forest School at Seattle's Washington Park Arboretum are outdoors for every minute of their four-hour school day. The nature-based program focuses on play and exploration. As children engage with the world around them, the staff supplements with curriculum to further engage their curiosity.
- Another preschool that embraced outdoor education was the subject of a blog and podcast: Outdoor Learning Leads to Curious Students. Riverside Nature School in Charles Town, West Virginia, was inspired by German Waldkindergarten schools.

Community Spaces

- The Maritime Discovery Schools is a districtwide place-based initiative in Port Townsend, Washington.

- The School of Environmental Studies, or "Zoo School," is on the grounds of the Minnesota Zoo in Apple Valley, Minnesota, and embraces project-based learning with an environmental theme. The school is a partnership between the city, the school district, and the zoo. In addition to studies at the zoo, SES students take excursions around the world to immerse students in new climates, cultures, and environmental issues.

- The Science and Math Institute at Point Defiance Zoo in Tacoma, Washington, partners with community resources to help create more inclusive learning experiences that educate the whole child and focus on the values of community, empathy, thinking, and balance.

Virtual Experiences

- Students at Winton Woods New Tech Network High School near Cincinnati, Ohio, created virtual reality World War I museum exhibits to immerse other students and teachers in the sights and sounds of war.

- Educators can use an app called Thinglink to design interactive place-based learning that incorporates virtual reality. Students can also tell digital stories about places with ThingLink's interactive image editor.

- Students at Parklands College in South Africa used a reality creation tool called CoSpaces to design a hypothetical eco-city. They based their virtual eco-city on an area of Cape Town formerly known as District Six, designing an urban area with a focus on sustainability and food security.

International Implementation

- La Paz Community School in Costa Rica is an incubator for effective place-based education strategies that promote cross-cultural competence in multilingual and multinational environments. The professional learning community at La Paz commits to focusing on the people and the place to create meaningful learning experiences.

- In Bhutan, a small country in the Himalayas between India and China, place-based learning with an emphasis on well-being and community health is growing. Teton Science Schools partners with the Royal Education Council and the Royal University of Bhutan to expand place-based education by linking place-based education principles with Bhutan's focus on what it calls "Gross National Happiness."

- In Finland, students spend nearly 80 percent of their time learning in the outdoors.

- Daguan Elementary School in Kunming, China, prepares students to become docents in a local history museum. After becoming experts in regional history, the students share this expertise with visitors.

- Dunrossness Primary School in Shetland, Scotland, maintains a relationship with the Crofting Connections, an organization that seeks to help children develop an awareness of Scottish agricultural and cultural traditions. The school includes a garden with a pond, hoop greenhouses that support the production of fruits and vegetables, and a meadow used for play and nature study. Local heritage is the focus throughout children's experience in the school.

A Review of Place-Based Education Principles

A great way to get started on a small scale is to review the design principles of place-based education and reflect on your existing practices. Do you already use some of these principles? If not, where is the easiest place to start? How might you try one of the action steps tomorrow or next week in your classroom? As a refresher, here are descriptions of the six principles.

- **Community as Classroom**: Communities serve as learning ecosystems for schools where local and regional experts, experiences, and places are part of the expanded definition of classroom.

- **Learner-Centered**: Learning is personally relevant to students and enables student agency.

- **Inquiry-Based**: Learning is grounded in observing, asking relevant questions, making predictions, and collecting data to understand the economic, ecological, and sociopolitical world.

- **Local to Global**: Local learning serves as a model for understanding global challenges, opportunities, and connections.

- **Design Thinking**: A systemic approach enables students to make a meaningful impact in communities through the curriculum.

- **Interdisciplinary**: The curriculum matches the real world in that the traditional subject-area content, skills, and dispositions are taught through an integrated, interdisciplinary, and frequently project-based approach in which all learners are accountable and challenged.

Place-Based Resources

A limited but excellent set of research articles and practical books about placed-based education have been written over the last three decades. The microsite (www.gettingsmart.com/placebasededucation) contains links to most of these resources, and the following guides are a great place to start:

- The Potential of Place-Based Education: This infographic details the potential outcomes of place-based education and how it connects learners to communities.
- Quick Start Guide to Place-Based Education: This guide outlines the big ideas of place-based education and ways to get started.
- Quick Start Guide to Place-Based Professional Learning: This guide is designed for educators who want to enhance their place-based practices and facilitation.
- What Is Place-Based Education and Why Does It Matter? This overview of place-based education includes summaries of the research behind it and findings about student outcomes.
- Giving the Gift of Place: Grab your headphones and take a virtual field trip to Murie Ranch in Grand Teton National Park to talk about place-based education with Christen Girard and Nate McClennen of Teton Science Schools.

Implementation

Figure 8.1 shows six phases of professional learning that are necessary for successful implementation of a place-based approach with your students (GettingSmart Staff, 2017). These can guide you as you build an implementation process tailored to the specific characteristics of your community. Let's look more closely at each of these phases.

Phase 1: Inquire into Place

In the first phase, educators develop a keen sense of wonder, appreciation, and understanding of their place—its history, economics, politics, ecology, cultures, social dynamics, and future. They can start by learning to authentically observe and ask questions around these aspects of place and by paying attention to local news, researching local history, exploring resources, hiking in the parks or woods, or talking to elders in the community. Through a personal process of inquiry, they begin to see their community as a potential classroom full of rich resources and possibilities to add context to student learning.

FIGURE 8.1. **Six Phases of Place-Based Professional Learning**

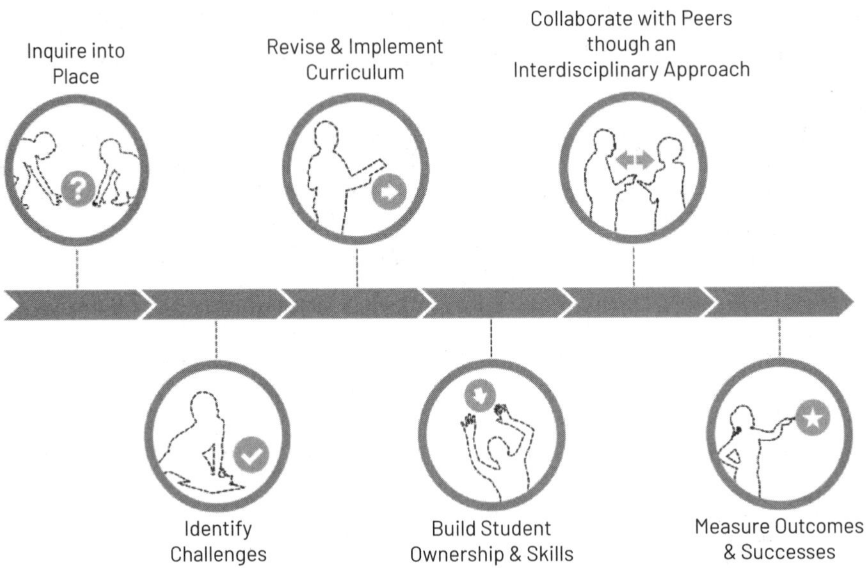

Activity: Find Your Connection to Place

The most powerful connections we make are when others are also engaged and committed to a topic or idea. But first you must experience the power of place for yourself. Get out into your community, reflect on a powerful place-based experience you had, and make connections for yourself. Use Figure 8.2 as a tool.

FIGURE 8.2. **Activity: Observing Place**

Directions: Pick a place in your community. Dedicate an hour to spend there. Use the following chart to reflect on your experience being in that place. Repeat this activity for as many places as needed or as are helpful. You can use this tool with students, too.

What was there (physical structures, people, places, things)?	What did you observe (see, hear, smell, consider)?	What content areas and topics could you connect to this place?	How might you integrate this place into your teaching?

Activity: Use a Self-Assessment and Observation Tool

Once you are ready, use the Teton Science Schools Rubric for Place-Based Implementation (Figure 8.3) to as a way to evaluate where you are in your own place-based practices and understandings.

Activity: Map Your Place

Understanding your own space and exploring it so you know it well helps give context to those people who are important in that place. How can you do this if you are new to an area or don't live in the immediate community of your school? You can use the two-part tool in Figure 8.4 to get started.

Before you undertake the first part, you can tap into student knowledge about the community. Students often know more about their community than they may realize. You can ask them about the places they frequent in the community—local stores, municipal buildings, parks, and other venues—and spend time getting to know those places yourself. Posting a community map in the classroom that students can contribute throughout the year is a great way to access student knowledge.

In the second part, strengths mapping, you will identify existing resources, places, and people that might be able to help you and your students in place-based experiences. Helpful asset-mapping tools and templates can be found at www.gettingsmart.com/placebasededucation.

Phase 2: Identify Challenges and Opportunities

The second phase of professional learning is to understand challenges that are faced by the community. Communities and places are dynamic, always struggling with change and adapting to new external and internal events. Understanding these challenges allows educators to understand the context at a deeper level. Educators must also accept the idea that that their students can be change agents. Design thinking is a way for students to systematically develop creative solutions to increase the community sustainability and vitality in the face of challenges.

Activity: Do Place-Based Research

Now that you have identified small entry points and ways to get started in understanding the community, dive deeper by conducting research and

FIGURE 8.3. Teton Science Schools Rubric for Place-Based Implementation

Directions: Rate your practice by marking your current level of implementation with an X in the appropriate box.

Principle	Level of Implementation				
Community as Classroom: Communities serve as learning ecosystems for schools, where local and regional experts, experiences, and places are part of the expanded definition of a classroom.	Learning is always inside the classroom, and no guests are invited in.	Learning occurs by interacting inside and outside the classroom with local places and partners for 1–5 days a year.	Learning occurs by interacting inside and outside the classroom with local places and partners for 6–10 days a year.	Learning occurs by interacting inside and outside the classroom with local places and partners for 10 or more days a year. Students study local challenges and present findings to local stakeholders or experts.	Learning occurs by interacting inside and outside the classroom with local places and partners at least 1 day a week. Students and community members build relationships to work and learn together.
Learner-Centered: Learning is personally relevant to students and enables student agency. The teacher serves as a guide or facilitator to learning.	Teacher delivers all content in the same way to the entire class and makes no intentional connections of learner to curriculum.	Teacher delivers all content but makes connections to the interests of learners.	Teacher designs and adjusts curriculum based on the needs of the individual students.	Teacher and students plan curriculum together, and learning is more personalized with knowledge of individual student interests in mind. Students understand the knowledge, skills, and dispositions required to successfully complete the curriculum.	Students are empowered to initiate and create curriculum that is relevant to the learner and with guidance from the teacher. Students can target the needed knowledge, skills, and dispositions appropriate for the current curriculum and the overall learning requirements.

Inquiry-Based: Learning is grounded in observing, asking relevant questions, making predictions, and collecting data to understand the world through economic, ecological, and cultural lenses. This approach allows for individual truth seeking based on evidence.	No inquiry is present in class.	Inquiry is introduced but not related to local/regional/global place.	Students can describe how to use the inquiry process to investigate a place, and the process is modeled for them in the curriculum.	Students use the inquiry process to investigate a place.	Students demonstrate how to use the inquiry process to comprehensively analyze the economic, ecological, and cultural components of a place.
Local to Global: Local learning serves as a model for understanding regional and global challenges, opportunities, and connections. An understanding of self is a starting point to understanding place.	Connections to regional and global context are not attempted.	Students learn about local, regional, or global concepts and issues in isolation, with no identified connection between the different scales of context.	Students learn about relationships between local, regional, and global concepts and issues in the classroom, and they are given some suggestions on how the different scales of context might relate.	Students learn about relationships between local, regional, and global concepts, and they explicitly learn that local and/or regional challenges relate to global concepts and challenges.	Students learn about relationships between local, regional, and global concepts and issues, and they make connections between themselves and the different scales of local, regional, and global contexts.

(continued)

FIGURE 8.3. Teton Science Schools Rubric for Place-Based Implementation (continued)

Principle	Level of Implementation				
Design Thinking: Design thinking provides a systematic approach for students to make a meaningful impact in communities through the curriculum.	Students are not presented, or do not discover, challenges based on a design process.	Students implement the design process to propose a solution to a teacher-determined problem.	Students implement the design process to propose a solution to a student-determined challenge.	Students implement the design process to solve a teacher-determined challenge that is connected to the local, regional, or global community.	Students implement the design process to solve a student-determined challenge that is connected to the local, regional, or global community.
Interdisciplinary: The curriculum is taught through an integrated and frequently project-based approach, in which all learners are accountable and challenged.	Content is presented as discrete disciplines and disconnected parts.	Content is presented with links to other disciplines, but they are not made explicit.	Content is presented with links to other disciplines, and students are prompted to explore how content connects across subject areas.	Connections between disciplines are emphasized, and students are expected to connect content across subject areas (project-based learning may be implemented).	Content is multidisciplinary and fully integrated through a project-based learning approach (often involving collaboration between teachers).

Source: Used with permission from Teton Science Schools, Jackson, WY.

FIGURE 8.4. **Activity: Mapping Your Place**

Part 1: Initial Community and Network Mapping

Community or Region:
Brief description:
Population:

Major Industries	Businesses	Education Organizations	Civic or Municipal Organizations	Religious Communities	Cultural or Historical Museums, Centers, Organizations
Parks and Outdoor Spaces	Free Services and Offerings	Landmarks, Statues, and Historical Sites	Music Venues or Performance Spaces	Newspapers or Media Outlets	[Add your own category.]

Part 2: Community Strengths Mapping

Choose one of the places, organizations, or people included in your initial mapping of the community. Note how you might work together in a place-based experience.

Place, Organization, or Person	Description	Value-Add or Strengths	How We Might Work Together

interviewing people in the places you've identified. You can do this yourself as part of your initial effort to understand the power of place, or with students once they are fully immersed in a place-based experience. Use some of the sample interview and research questions in Figure 8.5 to get started. Students can begin by interviewing their parents or caregivers.

FIGURE 8.5. **Activity: Place-Based Research and Interview Questions**

<u>General Questions</u>
- How does _____ [insert place name] affect or influence the community?
- What can we learn from exploring _____ [insert place name]?
- What would happen if _____ [insert place name] didn't exist? How would our community change?

<u>Questions Related to Place-Based Design Principles</u>

Community as Classroom
- How does our school connect to our local community?
- Whose stories are being told and whose are left behind? Why might that be the case? How might we rectify this situation?
- What are the cultural implications of _____ (e.g., a statue or monument)?

Learner-Centered
- What influence do I have on my community?
- How, and where, would I like to have an influence in my community?
- How do I identify with my community?
- How is my identity connected to my community?
- How might I use my interest in _____ [insert an interest] to _____ [insert a benefit or contribution]?
- Whose perspective do I need to understand better?

Local to Global
- How does our _____ [insert a behavior or issue—e.g., use of water, population growth, etc.] influence the world or other communities around the globe?
- Do any goods or services get exported from our community? Where do they go?

Inquiry-Based
- What do we observe in the natural world in our community?
- If we explore _____ [insert a place] for _____ [insert a period of time], what changes do we notice and what stays the same?
- How does _____ [insert a place-related person, place, or thing] play a role in the environment and ecosystem in _____ [insert a place]?

Design Thinking
- How might we uncover existing challenges or opportunities in our community?
- How can we design solutions for people in communities in which we live or seek to serve?
- How can we understand our own biases and empathize with others to determine the best opportunities for community innovation?

Interdisciplinary
- How are the places in this ecosystem connected? In what ways are _____, _____, _____ represented?
- What skills and knowledge were required by decision-makers in the community around a recent challenge?

<u>Place-Based Interview Questions</u>
Name of person being interviewed: _____
Your connection to that person (if any): _____
Person's place of work, or your reason for interviewing: _____
- Tell me about yourself.
- How did you get to this place?
- What is important about this place?
- What might not be readily observable about this place?
- Why should we care about this place?
- What challenges in this place are worth addressing?

Phase 3: Build, Revise, and Implement Learning Experiences

Once educators understand their place, it's time to connect their curriculum (one lesson, one standard, or one unit) to the place, using a variety of methods. By linking the unit or lesson to a tangible component of the local place, learning can begin with knowledge already acquired. It's best to begin with small steps in this redesign process, as it can be intimidating. Tools from project-based learning, Understanding by Design, Universal Design for Learning, and problem-based learning are good reference points. During this phase, it is also important to introduce risk management practices (e.g., introducing students to safety protocols when and if there is an emergency) to ensure safety for the students when you leave the classroom. Facilitating experiences outside the classroom walls takes attention and care—a responsibility that eventually needs to be taken on by students (see Phase 4).

Activity: Start Small

It is important to start small! As with any method or approach, it is advisable to begin with a reasonable task or idea before trying to totally revamp all of your practices. Here are steps you can follow:

1. Review the design principles and ways to take action (see the next section for a summary of these action steps).
2. Pick your entry point: Where do you want to start? What are your current strengths that you could build upon?
3. Try one of the action steps or map out how you might begin to address one of the design principles in your place-based practices. Use the template in Figure 8.6 as a guide and to track your progress. It includes examples for two of the design principles to get you thinking.

Phase 4: Build Student Ownership and Skills

After success with one or more teacher-led, place-based implementations, it's important to next develop increased student agency around both the inquiry and the design thinking components of the curriculum. Over time, students should begin to guide the experience by developing the core skills of inquiry and design, leadership competency, and risk management. The transfer of ownership should occur gradually, through levels of inquiry and levels of design that lead to increasing autonomy in students. The emerging knowledge base around learner-centered education is complementary to this phase.

FIGURE 8.6. **Activity: Starting Small with Design Principles**

Design Principle	Action Step or Entry Point	Short-Term Goal (4–6 Weeks)	Evidence of Progress	Next Steps
Learner-Centered	Introduce students to daily goal setting and reflection. What do they plan to do today, and what did they actually accomplish?	By the end of the period, students will write articulate, developmentally appropriate goals and concise reflections.	When asked, students share and demonstrate ownership over goals and reflections.	Students begin to assign their own homework (with teacher approval).
Inquiry	Students report on observations they make about the world on the way to school (weather, flora, fauna, traffic, etc.). Observations are documented weekly on the board and then transferred to a journal for long-term record keeping.	Students learn to be keen observers, reporting subtle and obvious changes in the world over a six-week period.	Students show indications of being more observant of long-term change through questions and observations across other learning experiences.	Begin to have students, rather than the teacher, document the observations.

Activity: Explore the Place Triangle

Have students build a personal and classroom version of the Place Triangle, as shown in Figure 8.7 (see Chapter 2, pp. 22–23, for more details on the triangle), by writing their answers to the questions, cutting magazine clippings that relate to the questions, creating artwork, and so on. For each section of the triangle, students can articulate observations or understandings and wonderings.

Phase 5: Find Peer or Community Partners

As educators become more comfortable implementing place-based education within their subject area or classroom, the next step is collaboration and cooperation with others to build the capacity for interdisciplinary learning

FIGURE 8.7. **Learner-Centered Place Triangle**

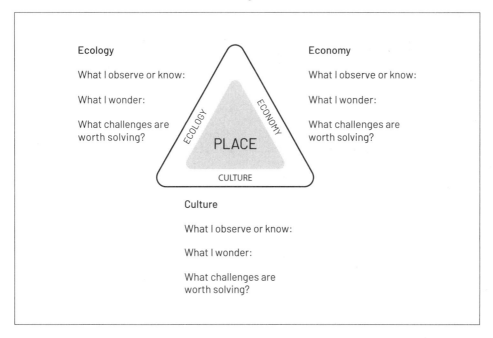

experiences. The challenges emerge around time and availability of resources; increased collaboration requires more flexibility in these areas. Changes to structures, such as the organization of schedules and courses, may be required. As in the earlier phases of professional learning and implementation, leadership skills remain critically important during this phase. As the implementation of place-based education broadens, teachers—like students—should attain increased levels of autonomy and agency.

Activity: Build a Community Partner Program

When working with community partners, a written agreement can help schools and teachers clearly articulate the expectations of the relationship. Figure 8.8 is an example that you can use as a guide.

Phase 6: Measure Outcomes and Share Successes

The final phase of professional learning is understanding and measuring desired outcomes. In the document *What Is Place-Based Education and Why Does It Matter?* (GettingSmart Staff, with eduInnovation and Teton Science

FIGURE 8.8. **Sample Agreement for a Community Partner Program Agreement**

School Contact:
Partner Organization:
Partner Contact:
Project Name: Sustainable Events Project
Project Goal(s): A local community foundation runs an annual event that includes a community meal, fun-run, and exhibition booths. As part of the commitment to sustainability, the foundation needs a way to measure the carbon footprint of the event. The goal of the project is to measure and report on the annual carbon footprint of the event.
School Commitments: As a school (specifically, a 10th grade math class), we commit to the following: • Collecting data during the event • Analyzing the data • Translating the data into carbon-footprint metrics • Reporting back to the organization in both presentation and written form
Partner Commitments: As a community partner, we commit to the following: • Providing an introductory presentation to students to describe the background and need (1 hour) • Providing access to required data or contacts to access the data • Acknowledging the student contribution in press release or other media releases • Reviewing draft of project and providing initial feedback (1 hour) • Meeting with students at school at the end of the project to review report and provide feedback (1 hour)
Signatures: _____ Project leader (school): _____ Project liaison (partner organization): _____

Schools, 2017), we noted that these outcomes include increased student engagement, improved learning outcomes, and positive community impact. Additional benefits include personalized learning, deeper learning, social-emotional learning, and improved motivation and persistence.

Educators can increase their capacity for research by using survey tools measuring student engagement, designing pre- and post-assessment tools, and comparing classrooms using the place-based approach with those that do not. Specifically, educators can design and execute action research projects around place-based education and report back to others who participated in the experience. They also can evaluate outcomes by identifying tangible changes in the community that emerge from the experiences, as reported by the students or those members of the community who have been affected by the change.

Activity: Conduct Action Research

Design and carry out an action research project (*Action Research* by Eileen Ferrance [2000] is a good introduction to the topic). Action research is an informal and quickly executed continuous-improvement tool that lets teachers practice the inquiry process. Data collected can be shared with colleagues or administrators—in addition to simply informing pedagogy. Action research can be used as part of a professional learning community (PLC) system within a school or district, with each teacher in the PLC implementing and sharing a project. You can use the template in Figure 8.9 to structure your action research.

Barriers

As we have mentioned at various times, educators may face certain roadblocks or barriers when they implement place-based education. We have seen many communities, including schools mentioned in this book, find ways to successfully navigate them. Among these barriers are the following:

- **Financial:** Arguably one of the chief barriers people express is concern about the lack of money to offer trips or place-based experiences to students. In this book we provide countless examples that do not require additional funding or a significant investment of time. With that said, we know that scholarships, grants, or other sources of financial support can help and are worth pursuing.

- **Safety:** In some communities, students and educators may not feel it is safe to explore and engage in place-based learning experiences. If safety is, in fact, a legitimate concern, consider bringing local experts to the school or having knowledgeable community leaders support place-based experiences (to have a higher teacher-to-student ratio).

- **School or community location:** "We live in the middle of nowhere, and no place here is interesting" is a common sentiment we have heard while researching place-based education. Another frequently heard comment is "I live in a city, and there are no outdoor spaces worth exploring." We disagree and believe that every community has outdoor opportunities worth taking advantage of if you dig deep enough.

- **Skills**: Educators in many schools are asked to focus solely on basic math and literacy skills as a way to raise test scores. At the root of this concern is usually a belief that greater priority should be placed on mastering basic academic skills. This sentiment—that students can't or don't have these

FIGURE 8.9. **Action Research Template**

Question and Topic of Investigation: (What are you studying? What parts of the placed-based education framework does it address?)	Place-Based Framework ☐ Interdisciplinary ☐ Learner-centered ☐ Local to global ☐ Community as classroom ☐ Inquiry ☐ Design thinking *Example:* Learner-Centered—Student voice in project direction
Hypothesis: (What do you predict will happen?)	*Example:* I predict that by asking students for input, they will be more engaged in the project and show a larger difference on pre/post assessments.
Rationale for the question/ problem: (Why did you choose this question or problem? How is it relevant to you and your teaching?)	*Example:* Basing learner experiences on prior knowledge and interest increases engagement and outcomes. When students have control over the direction, they are more responsible (Toshalis & Nakkula, 2012).
Methods: (How did you conduct your investigation? How did you collect your data?)	*Example:* I will run a mini project with two different groups of students who are randomly assigned to the group. One group will get a teacher-determined driving question, and the other will determine its own question. At the end of the unit, I will have students complete a basic engagement survey. Pre/post surveys will be completed to determine growth of students.
Results and Analysis: (What did you find? How can you share your findings with others in your school or the network?)	*Example:* My hypothesis was supported in terms of student engagement, but learning outcomes that I measured increased by the same amount in both groups.
Conclusions: (What is the conclusion of your research? What did you learn from this study?)	*Example:* Students' engagement increased so that they were more productive during the experience.
Action Plan: (Now that you have learned more about your teaching, what will you do with that information?	Example: I might consider measuring different items on my pre/post next time—for example, more skills than content.

Source: Used with permission from Teton Science Schools, Jackson, WY.

skills—also perpetuates inequalities that currently exist in schools today. However, place-based education experiences are an impactful way to integrate these skills into meaningful work and do not need to be considered "additional" lessons. Rather, they can be the math or literacy lessons themselves.

- **Permission:** Maximizing instructional time has been a focus in schools to ensure students are getting as much academics as they can. Teacher time is regulated by minute-to-minute daily schedules and learning blocks, and place-based education doesn't always fit in those structures. In these instances, an educator might present an alternative for how to combine subject areas to allow more time for place or demonstrate how place-based education experiences can work within the existing structures.

Stakeholder Starting Points

Anyone in a community can play a role in making place-based education a reality for students (including empowering the students themselves). Here are some suggested starting points for various stakeholders.

What Teachers Can Do

In addition to the previously mentioned ways to "start small" with place-based education, the following action steps (also listed at the end of the chapters discussing the respective design principles) are great ways to begin your place-based journey. This list is by no means exhaustive; nor are the steps listed in any particular order.

Community as Classroom

☐ **Explore your own place with family and friends.** Ask yourself the following questions: Who lives here now? Who lived here before? What drives the economy of this place? What are the ecological and geological systems at work in this place? Who holds power in this community? What are the current political issues? Is there inequity in this place?

☐ **Build a community map in your classroom or school.** Students of all ages can build community maps and add to them over multiple years. Specifying the location of projects, great partnerships, and community assets can remind teachers and students of community potential.

☐ **Create a community partnership program.** Begin by creating a formal document that outlines the benefits the organization will have by partnering with the school (and vice versa). Identify your strongest informal partners and ask one of them to act as a pilot community partner. Include them in school communications, share annual results, and celebrate successful projects. Over time, you will build more partners interested in investing in students' learning experience.

☐ **Survey your parent body for "challenges worth addressing."** Create a brief survey to send to parents or community members to discover community needs. Post the results in the classroom or in a larger school space, and check off those challenges that the class has addressed. Repeat the process annually to expand the list of potential projects.

☐ **Take your students out of the classroom.** Start simply. Take them on a walking tour of the school to observe the economic, ecological, and cultural components. Build leadership capacity from the start by asking students what leaving the classroom should look like and how they want to represent themselves. End by having the students brainstorm potential opportunities for place-based experiences that exist within the school building or campus.

☐ **Write a digital community newspaper with your students.** Simple digital tools such as the online media platforms Medium and Blogger make it easy to create and post news stories. Students can move beyond the typical classroom paper to write real articles about real issues in the community and make them public from the start. The authenticity will matter to the students, and the resource, especially in smaller towns where local newspapers are no longer sustainable, could be welcomed.

☐ **Visit local historical sites.** Boston Public Schools created place-based resources that help educators when they are exploring local historical sites ("BPS Place-Based Learning Opportunities," n.d.). Schools have started to move beyond typical field trips and incorporate more ongoing place-based experiences.

☐ **Do a community deep dive.** At Teton Science Schools in northwest Wyoming and eastern Idaho, high school students look through the lens of the Place Triangle (Figure 2.1, p. 23) to understand community sustainability. They complete a deep-dive inquiry into the issue using an approach that integrates social studies, science, economics, visual arts, and English.

☐ **Take advantage of internships.** Students enrolled in the national network of Big Picture Learning schools are out in internships with adults two full days a week, implementing the Community as Classroom principle. The experience builds social capital along with a host of other knowledge, skills, and dispositions ("Big Picture Learning," n.d.).

☐ **Consider joint facilities.** e3 Civic High and the downtown San Diego Central Library are housed in the same building. The library and community are brought directly to the school and vice versa. The Math and Science Institute, a high school in Tacoma, Washington, is located within the Port Defiance Zoo and Aquarium. Students engage in place-based projects around zoology. Here are a few additional examples of joint facilities:

— Houston A+ Unlimited Potential is located inside the Houston Museum of Natural Science. Students regularly engage with museumgoers (as docents) and workers (by collaborating on exhibit design).

— Gary Comer College Prep, a high school in Chicago's Noble Network, located with a youth center, has rooftop gardens and community gardens across the street.

— Thrive Public Schools' new K–8 campus in the Linda Vista neighborhood of San Diego is located with the Bayside Community Center.

— Roscoe Independent School District in Texas hosts businesses within the district's high school building, including businesses providing drone technology and veterinary services.

Learner-Centered

☐ **Encourage leadership opportunities and student-formed committees.** When immersed in a sense of place, students start to feel strong conviction and connections to causes or issues in their communities or elsewhere. They latch onto causes they care about and initiatives that matter most to them and their communities. Student-formed committees and leadership opportunities are a great way to deepen student engagement and motivation. Students lead the board of directors at the nonprofit organization One Stone in Boise, Idaho, and have created their own committees based on projects tied to local challenges.

☐ **Conduct student-led conferences.** Teacher-student conferences that are actually led by the student are a great way to get started with learner-centered practices, and they can reveal key insights about our teaching as well. Student-led conferences can reveal where needs are and are not being met, how a student likes to learn, and where there are opportunities for growth. They also provide an opportunity for students to divulge place-based experiences they've had that made an impact on them, as well as those that they'd like to have. When students share their thoughts about their learning, engagement increases as well as ownership and agency (Share Your Learning, n.d.).

☐ **Use competency-based report cards.** Redesign learning around competencies and incorporate them into student report cards. Many schools are using portfolios in conjunction with mastery-based transcripts. Check out the website of the Mastery Transcript Consortium (https://mastery.org), a network of schools that are working together to create "a high school transcript that reflects the unique skills, strengths, and interests of each learner."

☐ **Create a "genius hour."** Well established in many schools, a genius hour is a time for students to explore any topic, in any way. Create a high level of accountability by linking the explorations to the set of skills required by the school—especially those related to collaboration, communication, and creativity.

☐ **Make daily goals and reflection a habit.** Build a habit of students writing daily goals around standards or learning targets and reflecting on those goals. Over time they will easily answer the questions "Where have I learned?" "What am I learning?" and "What am I learning next?"

☐ **Move toward more self-directed learning.** At New Harmony High School in New Orleans, the school's vision statement emphasizes place and learner-centeredness in its opening sentences: "New Harmony High School empowers each student to actively direct their own learning. As our name suggests, students will work to find new harmonies in order to restore balance that has been lost in our coastal communities, finding new ways of sustaining ourselves in an uncertain future" (New Harmony High School, n.d., para. 1). They simply state, "School is Everywhere." Students engage in projects that connect them to their community. They view most projects through the lens of what is going on in the coastal region and what is being done to preserve the land. In addition to their teachers, students work alongside community members, mentors, and local experts.

Inquiry-Based

☐ **Incorporate big data and data analysis sprints.** Challenge students to ask questions around big-data sets. Have them dig deep to analyze data around complex topics using resources such as the search engine Wolfram Alpha; data tools developed by the nonprofit organization Gapminder; and the database and website Chronicling America, which provides access to historic newspaper articles. Students can use tools such as Data USA to analyze and investigate megatrends, cities, population growth, and other place-based topics of interest throughout their inquiry process.

☐ **Take a walk.** Especially with younger students, guide them along a sidewalk or take them to a park or other open space and provide quiet time for them to make observations and ask questions.

☐ **Use survey tools.** Jim Bentley, a National Geographic Educator and current practicing teacher, uses tools such as Survey123 to engage students in inquiring about different places near and far. He encourages students to use tools that might not be designed specifically for K–12 classrooms but that they might use in the real world. For example, there are apps that help students gather, analyze, and understand their data in order to make the best decisions.

☐ **Set up question walls.** Designate a space in your learning area or classroom for posting student- and teacher-generated questions that emerge throughout the year. These questions can be the inspiration for future inquiry.

☐ **Use classroom openers.** Begin each day with a photo, video, or object and have students ask related questions. Repeated practice develops the ability to ask powerful questions that can begin an inquiry.

☐ **Assign mini research projects.** After students understand and know how to use inquiry tools, have them carry out an individual, original research project. Even young students can ask questions and collect data that are relevant. By owning the project from start to finish, students build agency around the inquiry process.

☐ **Engage students in phenology.** Phenology relates to the influence of climate on such annual phenomena as plant budding and animal migrations. Have students track observations of the natural (and possibly human-built) world around them. They can create a monthly tracker on the wall to report their observations by day, week, month, or season. For example, they can report on birds observed, weather patterns, leaf color, moon cycle, or other natural phenomena. Helping students become more observant helps them become better at inquiry.

❏ **Ask students to share questions they have about their community.** High-quality projects and student work are often driven by a question that they generate.

❏ **Participate in interdisciplinary educator experiences.** Organizations such as the Wellborn Hub, the ECO Institute at the North Branch Nature Center in Vermont, the Teacher Learning Center at Teton Science Schools in Wyoming, and the Center for Place-Based Education at Antioch University New England offer place-based experiences for educators, helping them develop their understanding of the inquiry process. For example, as described on its website (https://northbranchnaturecenter.org/eco-institute), the ECO Institute "provides week-long, nature immersion courses for teachers, assistants, and administrators. The Institute is inquiry-based, outdoor learning through intensive experiential lessons, activities, and discussions" (ECO Institute, n.d.).

Local to Global

❏ **Build a Local to Global news wall.** Have students bring in national and international news articles and add to a Local to Global wall where they can make concrete connections to local and regional phenomena. For example, they may discover that global steel prices affect compensation at a local steel factory, or that the existence of recycling programs depends on global demand for recycled goods.

❏ **Create a digital community newspaper.** Using simple technology tools, build a local news blog run exclusively by students. To cover English language arts targets, require that each student write one article a year about the local community. Promote the newspaper to parents to encourage a local following.

❏ **Create a virtual reality experience.** Build a local tour of your community focused on the three aspects of the Place Triangle (see Figure 2.1, p. 23) and share it via technology such as the Google Cardboard device. Find other schools across the globe to share with.

- [ ] **Connect to a global opportunity.** List global problems worth solving or refer to the UN's 17 Sustainable Development Goals. Have students link projects and tasks to these goals in a classroom display.

- [ ] **Build a learning community in your region.** Using an effort by LRNG, Chicago Cities of Learning, and Aurora Public Schools as an example, pilot a small, community badging program that allows community organizations to post playlists, experiences, and challenges worth solving, and have students sign up and receive credit for completing these opportunities.

- [ ] **Connect virtually with another school.** Partner with another school to solve a common challenge (perhaps through the design thinking process described in Chapter 6).

- [ ] **Study exports and imports.** Have students investigate your community to determine inflows and outflows and identify if the community is a net exporter or net importer. Challenge students to identify possibilities for local production and micro-manufacturing to connect to the larger economic system.

- [ ] **Try a project with a global-issue focus and make local connections.** An increasing number of project-based learning examples are available online, including some from PBLWorks, CraftEd Curriculum, and EL Education. See, for example, the Think Globally, Act Locally example from PBLWorks and adapt materials and instruction as needed.

- [ ] **Connect globally to gain intercultural understandings.** Schools across the United States and around the world are connecting with each other to deepen intercultural understandings and levels of students' global competence, using tools such as Skype and Empatico (Lindsay, 2017). Connecting to collaborate on projects, share perspectives on similar topics, or just to have social exchanges is a great way to begin local-to-global place-based work in your classroom.

Design Thinking

- [ ] **Conduct community opportunity surveys.** Survey parents and community members to identify real need in the community. Have students review and select challenges to address through place-based projects.

- [ ] **Rethink the classroom.** Introduce design thinking methodology to redesign the classroom learning space (walls, furniture, etc.).

- [ ] **Create mini makerspaces.** Create a mini makerspace in your classroom that allows students to build and make things using simple supplies.

- [ ] **Present design challenges.** Present weekly or monthly design challenges for students to complete independently.

- [ ] **Embed the design thinking process in decision making.** Build anchor charts for the classroom around design thinking so that it becomes a common problem-solving tool (see IDEO, www.ideo.com, or d.school, https://dschool.stanford.edu, for tool collections).

- [ ] **Have students generate challenges worth solving.** Create a space in the classroom where students can post challenges of interest to them.

- [ ] **Support a student-run business.** At One Stone, a high school in Boise, Idaho, students run a marketing and design firm called Two Birds, interacting with adults at all levels of the business. Students take adults through the design thinking process and use it in their own work. Throughout the process they consider context and place as key factors for whatever they design and create for their clients. Many schools across the United States are partnering with Real World Scholars and, through their EdCorps program, are empowering students to create their own businesses.

- [ ] **Connect with industry to create.** At e3 Civic High in San Diego and Vista Innovation and Design Academy in Vista, California, students use the design thinking process, especially focusing on the element of empathy, to cocreate meaningful place-based projects with industry partners (Liebtag, 2017c). Partners include local libraries, large technology corporations, and hospitals, all of which have human-centered design challenges that they want students to help them tackle. E3 students work over the course of six months on projects to "engage, educate and empower scholars to solve personalized complex problems that positively impact local and/or global communities" (e3 Civic High, n.d.).

Interdisciplinary

- [ ] **Build your first project.** Do you teach only one subject and find it difficult to envision how you might facilitate an interdisciplinary project? Start with a unit you have taught in the past or a previous lesson and try to identify how you could have students elaborate on a particular aspect by incorporating another discipline. Use tools like the CraftED PBL Planning Guide or the Project Planner from PBLWorks to get started.

❏ **Meld place-based learning into coplanning across disciplines.** Are you already working across disciplines or coteaching? Try to coplan a project in which standards and objectives traverse subject areas *and* engage students in some form of place-based learning.

❏ **Develop interdisciplinary driving questions.** Work with colleagues and students to craft driving questions that naturally lend themselves to multiple subject areas or disciplines. You can use existing driving questions as starting points.

❏ **Seek authentic partners and audiences.** Do an asset map of your immediate school and local communities. Who can students work with to enhance their work? Instead of relying on those who frequently volunteer or otherwise contribute, get creative in identifying potential allies. We have seen interdisciplinary place-based projects in which students worked with local stores, universities, nonprofits, and government agencies.

❏ **Visit another classroom.** In person or virtually, visit another classroom that is doing this work well. Schools featured in this book welcome invitations to learn together. You can also search #placebaseded on Twitter for possible connections. Learn from and with these educators about their interdisciplinary place-based learning environments.

❏ **Explore place-based postsecondary programs.** Programs such as CITYterm (www.cityterm.org) and Minerva (www.minerva.kgi.edu) offer students and adults place-based postsecondary learning experiences. Students who may not have had the opportunity to live and learn in a city or a rural part of the world can experience a different way of living, learn about varied cultures, and gain new networks and opportunities, all while learning multiple subject areas and content. Elizabeth Irvin, a high school student at the time, shared her thoughts about her place-based experience in New York City:

> I feel like my experience with place-based education prepared me to thrive in every aspect of my being, and in turn, has influenced my life post-CITYterm. By immersing myself

fully in this style of learning, I was able to uncover new academic interests that I may hope to pursue as a career. (Irvin, 2018, para. 6)

What Policymakers Can Do

- ❑ **Consider weighted funding.** School board members and school leaders, if serious about equity and place, should explore the possibility of weighted student funding—that is, funding based on student need. Such funding can support place-based experiences for *all* students.

- ❑ **Seek financial support.** Ask local and national foundations and organizations to allocate portions of their funds to place-based learning in the community. Many community-based organizations are dedicated to supporting local issues and groups.

- ❑ **Do a policy refresh.** Eliminate policies that inhibit place-based experiences, including those that limit use of public vehicles, put constraints on where students are allowed to travel during the school day, and the like. Many outdated policies support traditional school models instead of encouraging forward-thinking learning experiences and responding to changes in the world.

- ❑ **Revise master schedules.** Explore how schedules and calendars can be changed to support place-based experiences and longer periods of inquiry during the regular school day. For example, many schools have designated instructional blocks for each subject area. High-quality place-based experiences are richer when students have more time to explore and dive deeply into topics, and because these experiences often encompass multiple subject areas, longer instructional periods and coteaching make sense.

- ❑ **Review transportation budgets.** Consider how to change transportation budgets to support trips and excursions. In urban school districts, seek options to provide access to public transit or free passes for students.

- ❑ **Tap into community assets.** Support community partnerships and leverage existing networks to highlight how people outside the school can play a critical role in their town's educational ecosystem. When schools are seen as a resource for the community, the potential for collaborations and contributions are limitless. To reinforce positive perceptions, students can assist with community research and help with actual civic projects (Smith, 2016).

What Parents or Guardians Can Do

☐ **Get connected.** Investigate your city or town and find ways to get involved. Share how you are doing this with your children.

☐ **Share your experience.** Call your child's teacher and share what you know about the community and the people within it. Volunteer your expertise as a member of the community.

☐ **Tell your story.** Tell your children about your place and why it is important. Storytelling is an important tool for all cultures, across multiple generations.

☐ **Listen to your child's stories about place.** Children explore place in many ways and build their own experience. Ask them about their discoveries.

☐ **Talk with teachers.** Figure out how teachers are integrating place into student learning and how you might incorporate your own understanding of place into the school community.

What Students Can Do

☐ **Get outside.** Explore! Find a friend and build an adventure—whether to the local store, park, street corner, or backyard. If you do not feel comfortable venturing into your immediate neighborhood, connect with and explore places on a smartphone or other device. If you don't have access to one, check out a local library or location that offers free access.

☐ **Unpack equity.** Understand the diverse backgrounds in your community and how you interact in places within your town, city, or ecosystem.

☐ **Tell your story.** Whose story is being told, and what stories are not being told? Get into your community and tell your story. Students as young as 2nd graders have been telling their stories in Cajon Valley Unified School District through a program called TEDxKids@ElCajon (www.tedxkidselcajon.com).

☐ **Advocate for your interests.** Share your interests with your teachers, your parents or guardians, local leaders, and others. The more you share your voice and get connected, the more people you will have as advocates for your interests and your desire to engage in place-based education. Some may think it is unrealistic to ask students to advocate for themselves, but we have seen it done. Student voice, especially in systems that marginalize some parts of community, is a powerful tool for justice and equity.

☐ **Complete an asset map.** Identify who in your community you know and who you'd like to get to know. Use tools such as the Mapping Your Place template (Figure 8.4, p. 111).

What Schools Can Do

☐ **Find networks and models.** Networks are powerful ways to amplify and accelerate progress in place-based implementation at schools. Place Network Schools is an example of a network that supports schools in the implementation of a next-generation place-based education model. Other examples include EL Education, which focuses on project-based learning, and Big Picture Learning Network, which focuses on internships.

☐ **Commit to long-term implementation.** Avoid the "one-hit wonder" model of adoption. Build the rationale behind place-based education and embed it deeply into strategic plans.

☐ **Reach out to partner schools.** Find out who is already implementing place-based education in your region. Send teachers and administrators to visit and learn from others.

☐ **Build an "innovation" mindset in your school.** Create an environment of trust and cultivate an innovation mindset, one that acknowledges failure and encourages pilots as part of the long-term process leading to success.

☐ **Measure and celebrate results.** Develop assessments and measurements that reflect place-based principles and the value of community engagement in student work.

☐ **Find funding sources.** Outside of professional development funds, school leaders can reach out to local and national philanthropic organizations, community foundations, and school foundations to support important work.

Epilogue

Every individual matters. Every individual has a role to play. Every individual makes a difference.

—**Jane Goodall,** anthropologist

"We're living with the excesses of 60 years of hyper individualism," argues author and columnist David Brooks (2019, para. 10). "There's a lot of emphasis in our culture on personal freedom, self-interest, self-expression, the idea that life is an individual journey toward personal fulfillment. You do you."

Brooks argues there are "rippers," those who tear social fabric, and "weavers," those who "share an ethos that puts relationship over self." Educators appreciate that we are born into relationships, that we learn in relationships, and that we grow in community. As Brooks says, "We precedes me."

Introducing children to the place they are from is weaving community. Introducing young people to other places builds empathy and understanding— a quilt of communities.

With its inherent complexity, place as pedagogy frames experiences that are uniquely efficient at delivering priority outcomes—agency, equity, and community. Place is also an ethic, a mindset of appreciating and caring for places near and far. Place calls us to contribute, to situate the benefit we leave behind.

As pedagogy and ethic, the cross-cutting concepts in the Next Generation Science Standards—cause and effect; scale, proportion, and quantity; systems and system models; energy and matter; structure and function; and stability and change—invite young people into place to identify patterns, see connections, and begin to understand complex systems.

KEEN (the Kern Entrepreneurship Education Network) is a network of 40 universities committed to teaching engineers to spot opportunity and create impact—what they call "an entrepreneurial mindset." Place-based learning develops the same impulse of opportunity and impact. An individual with a place mindset asks: What are my obligations to this place? What can this place teach me? In what way can I contribute to this place? As we enter place together, we may ask: What do we owe this place? What can it teach us? How may we serve as good ancestors?

> "Imagine a leap from our current self to our emerging future Self. We are facing that threshold, gap, chasm or abyss on all levels of scale: as individuals, groups, organizations, and as a global community. How can we activate our deeper levels of humanity in order to bridge and cross that divide?"
> —C. Otto Scharmer, 2016, p. xvii

We are several decades into a great acceleration of the Anthropocene, the geologic epoch of human impact. We are also several years into a new innovation economy augmented by artificial intelligence. The collision of complex manmade and natural systems is producing unprecedented events and mounting existential risks.

Paradoxically, the pace of scientific discovery, the development of augmented intelligence, and the power of entrepreneurial ecosystems will produce unimaginable benefit in the coming decades: diseases will be eradicated, climate solutions will be developed, transportation will become safer and cheaper, and extraordinary wealth will be produced.

Regional and national governments are facing cascading waves of complex issues that strain civic capacity. These issues—including implications of artificial intelligence, how we care for our environment and for each other—call for a new ethical framework and a more agile civic infrastructure. The future will be what we decide to share—the wealth and the benefits created, and the places we cohabit.

Despite mounting risks, the second decade of the 21st century is a wonderful time to be a young person on this planet. It has never been easier to make a difference by coding an application, harnessing smart tools, launching a campaign, or starting an organization that will have a positive impact on the world. Many of these meaningful contributions will be community connected—the result of an adult working in relationship with a young person and a place.

Encouraged by the thousands of communities adopting broader educational goals—including agency, equity, and community—we hope to see more elementary and secondary schools embrace the six design principles of place-based education. We hope to see more partnerships that treat the community as classroom. We hope to see more schools come alive with a sense of possibility.

"Renewal is building, relationship by relationship, community by community," says Brooks. "It will spread and spread as the sparks fly upward" (2019, para. 21).

Whether you are an educator, a parent, a student, or a civic or business leader, start small, but start *now*. Try something, then do it again and make it better. Invite others to join, weave community, and advocate for equity. Young people are craving the potential connections that can be made through place-based experiences. Your community deserves the benefits that derive from those connections.

> "We live in an age of disruption. Any review of the underlying driving forces will convince us that the rate of disruption will continue to go up, not down. It's too late to reverse several of these forces and trends. So if we cannot control the rate of exterior disruption, what, if anything, can we control?
>
> The only thing we can really control or shape is our interior response: how we show up when disruption hits. . . . The future of our social systems, societies, and the planet as a whole depends in no small way on the choices we make in these moments."
>
> **—C. Otto Scharmer,** 2016, p. 28

Glossary

Blended learning: Learning in which a student learns, at least in part, at a supervised brick-and-mortar location away from home and, at least in part, through online delivery with some element of student control over time, place, path, and/or pace. The modalities along each student's learning path within a course or subject are connected to provide an integrated learning experience (Christensen, Staker, & Horn, 2013).

Competency-based education: A shift from time-based milestones to learning-based milestones as drivers in education (also called mastery-based, proficiency-based, and performance-based) (Getting Smart, n.d., p. 3).

Deeper learning: Popularized by the William and Flora Hewlett Foundation, deeper learning experiences contribute to the development of skills and knowledge that students must possess to succeed in 21st-century jobs and civic life, including (1) mastering core academic content, (2) thinking critically and solving complex problems, (3) working collaboratively, (4) communicating effectively, (5) learning how to learn, and (6) developing academic mindsets (William and Flora Hewlett Foundation, 2013, p. 1).

Design thinking: Attacking complex problems with empathy and iteration, using a structured process with the aim of approaching a desired goal, target, or result. The Hasso Plattner Institute of Design at Stanford (d.school) has developed a model with five stages: Empathize, Define, Ideate, Prototype, and Test.

Personalized learning: Tailoring learning for each student's strengths, needs, and interests—including enabling student voice and choice in what, how, when, and where they learn—to provide flexibility and supports to ensure mastery of the highest standards possible (Powell, Kennedy, & Patrick, 2013, p. 4).

Place-based education: Anytime, anywhere learning that leverages the power of place to personalize learning.

Project-based learning: A multistep activity that incorporates authenticity, intellectual challenge, collaboration, project management, public product, and reflection (High Quality Project Based Learning, n.d., para. 5).

Student-centered learning: There are four key tenets of student-centered approaches that are essential to students' full engagement in achieving deeper learning outcomes, which are identified by the Nellie Mae Education Foundation (2014, p. 3), the leading champion of student-centered learning. They are (1) learning is personalized; (2) learning is competency-based; (3) learning takes place anytime, anywhere; and (4) students exert ownership over their learning.

References

Abel, N. (2016, February 17). What is personalized learning? [blog post]. Retrieved from *iNACOL* at www.inacol.org/news/what-is-personalized-learning

Allen, D. (2017, August 10). Our journey to the XQ—Key design elements of Círculos [blog post]. Retrieved from *#schoolmadefresh* at https://schoolmadefresh.wordpress .com/2017/08/10/our-journey-to-the-xq-key-design-elements-of-circulos

Anderson, S. (2018, July 10). Place-based education: Think globally, teach locally [blog post]. Retrieved from *EdWeek* at https://blogs.edweek.org/edweek/global_learning /2018/07/place-based_education_think_globally_teach_locally.html

Andrews, X. (2018, July 31). First semester of Intrepid Academy at Hale. Retrieved from www.bostonpublicschools.org

Banchi, H., & Bell, R. (2008). The many levels of inquiry [blog post]. Retrieved from *Thinking, Learning and Teaching* at http://tltjc.blogspot.com/2011/02/banchi-and -bell-2008-four-levels-of.html

Barron, A. (2017, March 23). Why we use digital badges at Del Lago Academy [blog post]. Retrieved from *Getting Smart* at www.gettingsmart.com/2017/03/why-we-use -digital-badges-at-del-lago-academy

Big Picture Learning. (n.d.). Home page. Retrieved from www.bigpicture.org

Boggs School. (n.d. a). Mission and core ideology. Retrieved from www.boggsschool.org /mission-core-ideology

Boggs School. (n.d. b). Place-based education. Retrieved from www.boggsschool.org /place-based-education

BPS Place-Based Learning. (n.d.). BPS place-based learning opportunities. Retrieved from https://sites.google.com/bostonpublicschools.org/placebasedlearning

Brooks, D. (2019, February 18). A nation of weavers. *The New York Times*. Retrieved from www.nytimes.com/2019/02/18/opinion/culture-compassion.html

Charlot, J., Leck, C., & Saxberg, B. (2018). *Designing for learning: A primer on key insights from the science of learning and development*. Retrieved from https://static1.squarespace.com/static/55ca46dee4b0fc536f717de8/t/5be841ac4d7a9c5e1eeea528/1541948239807/Designing+for+Learning+Primer+Transcend.pdf

Chicago Tech Academy. (n.d.). Vision and mission. Retrieved from https://chitech.org/mission/

Christensen, C., Staker, H., & Horn, M. B. (2013, May 22). Is K–12 blended learning disruptive? An introduction to the theory of hybrids. Retrieved from www.christenseninstitute.org/publications/hybrids

Christenson, S. L. (2013). *Handbook of research on student engagement.* New York: Springer.

Colburn, A. (2000). *An inquiry primer.* Retrieved from www.experientiallearning.ucdavis.edu/module2/el2-60-primer.pdf

Columbus, L. (2017, December 11). LinkedIn's fastest-growing jobs today are in data science and machine learning. *Forbes.* Retrieved from www.forbes.com/sites/louiscolumbus/2017/12/11/linkedins-fastest-growing-jobs-today-are-in-data-science-machine-learning/#66ad7bbe51bd

Convergence. (2018). *A transformational vision for education in the U.S.* Retrieved from https://education-reimagined.org/wp-content/uploads/2019/01/Vision_Website.pdf

Davis, E., Rae, A., & Leite, S. (2017, January 30). Preparing #LifeReady students: Creating globally-sourced, locally-relevant curriculum [blog post]. Retrieved from *Getting Smart* at www.gettingsmart.com/2017/01/creating-globally-sourced-locally-relevant-curriculum

Deardorff, D. K. (2009). *The SAGE handbook of intercultural competence.* Los Angeles: Sage.

Delpit, L. D. (2012). *"Multiplication is for white people": Raising expectations for other people's children.* New York: New Press.

De Palma, L. D. (2017, December 6). The Boggs School oral history project: Linking youth and elders to the past, present and future [blog post]. Retrieved from *Huffington Post* at www.huffingtonpost.com/laura-m-de-palma/the-boggs-school-celebrates-oral-history-project_b_6337808.html

Dewey, J. (n.d.). School and society. Retrieved from https://brocku.ca/MeadProject/Dewey/Dewey_1907/Dewey_1907c.html

d.school. (n.d.). Equity-centered design framework. Retrieved from https://dschool.stanford.edu/resources/equity-centered-design-framework

e3 Civic High (n.d.) Design thinking community class. Retrieved from www.e3civichigh.com/apps/pages/index.jsp?uREC_ID=206559&type=d&pREC_ID=1166143

ECO Institute. (n.d.). Home page. Retrieved from https://northbranchnaturecenter.org/eco-institute

Education Reimagined. (2018). *Practitioner's lexicon: What is meant by key terminology.* Washington DC: Author. Retrieved from https://education-reimagined.org/wp-content/uploads/2018/03/Revised-Lexicon_Jan2018_DOWNLOAD.pdf

Education Reimagined. (2019, January 30). Education Reimagined Symposium 2019: Stories of impact Carlos Moreno [video file]. Retrieved from https://vimeo.com/314391698

Education Reimagined. (n.d.). Chugach School District. Retrieved from https://education-reimagined.org/map/chugach-school-district

EL Education. (n.d.). History. Retrieved from https://eleducation.org/who-we-are /history

El Paso Independent School District (EPISD) and New Tech Network. (2018). *El Paso Schools: How the New Tech Network partnership accelerated progress.* Retrieved from www.gettingsmart.com/wp-content/uploads/2018/09/EPISD-NTNStory -2018Sept11v4.pdf

Embarc Chicago. (n.d.). Home page. Retrieved from www.embarcchicago.org

Erickson, H. L. (2007). *Concept-based curriculum and instruction for the thinking classroom.* Thousand Oaks, CA: Corwin.

Ferguson, R. F., Phillips, S. F., Rowley, J. F., & Friedlander, J. W. (2015). *The influence of teaching: Beyond standardized test scores: Engagement, mindsets, and agency.* Retrieved from www.agi.harvard.edu/projects/TeachingandAgency.pdf

Ferrance, E. (2000). *Action research.* Providence, RI: LAB at Brown University. Retrieved from www.brown.edu/academics/education-alliance/sites/brown.edu.academics .education-alliance/files/publications/act_research.pdf

Fisher, J. F. (2015, March 26). The invisible currency in education reform: Social capital [blog post]. Retrieved from *Christensen Institute* at www.christenseninstitute.org /blog/the-invisible-currency-in-education-reform-social-capital

Fisher, J. F., & Fisher, D. (2018). *Who you know: Unlocking innovations that expand students' networks.* San Francisco: Jossey-Bass.

Getting Smart. (n.d.). Show what you know: A landscape analysis of competency-based education. Retrieved from https://xqsuperschool.org/competency-based -education-cbe/part1

Getting Smart. (2018a). *Ace Leadership High School case study 2018.* Retrieved from https://hqpbl.org/wp-content/uploads/2018/02/HQPBL-CaseStudy-ACE.pdf

Getting Smart. (2018b). *Albemarle County Public Schools case study 2018.* Retrieved from https://hqpbl.org/wp-content/uploads/2018/03/HQPBL-CaseStudy-Albemarle.pdf

Getting Smart. (2019). Podcast: Greg Smith on climate collapse [blog post]. Retrieved from *Getting Smart* at www.gettingsmart.com/2019/07/podcast-greg-smith-on-a -powerful-sense-of-place

Getting Smart Staff. (2017, March 2). Quick start guide to place-based professional learning [blog post]. Retrieved from *Getting Smart* at www.gettingsmart.com/2017/03 /place-based-professional-learning

Getting Smart Staff. (2018a, January 17). High tech exec advocates for high agency learning [blog post]. Retrieved from *Getting Smart* at www.gettingsmart.com/2018/01 /high-tech-exec-advocates-for-high-agency-learning

Getting Smart Staff. (2018b, February 9). Whittle School and Studios: Transforming education for global good [blog post]. Retrieved from *Getting Smart* at www.gettingsmart.com/2018/02/whittle-school-studios-transforming-education

Getting Smart Staff. (2019, February 20). Learner-centered Iowa BIG propels Jemar Lee [blog post]. Retrieved from *Getting Smart* at www.gettingsmart.com/2019/02 /learner-centered-iowa-big-propels-jemar-lee

Getting Smart Staff, with eduInnovation and Teton Science Schools. (2017). *What is place-based education and why does it matter?* Retrieved from www.gettingsmart.com /wp-content/uploads/2017/02/What-is-Place-Based-Education-and-Why-Does-it -Matter-3.pdf

Hartford Heritage Project. (n.d.). Home page. Retrieved from www.capitalcc.edu/hhp

High Quality Project Based Learning. (n.d.). Home page. Retrieved from https://hqpbl.org

Hill, E. (2017, April 7). What a Rhode Island teen wants you to know about her year in the Middle East: "Every culture has beauty." *People.* Retrieved from https://people.com /human-interest/rhode-island-teen-met-school-middle-east

Holland, B. (2019, January 24). Reggio Emilia: The future of learning has roots in the past [blog post]. Retrieved from *Getting Smart* at www.gettingsmart.com/2019/01 /reggio-emilia-the-future-of-learning-has-roots-in-the-past

IDEO. (n.d.). IDEO is a global design and innovation company. Retrieved from www.ideo.com/about

InnovateBPS. (n.d.) Intrepid Academy at Hale. Retrieved from https://sites.google.com /bostonpublicschools.org/innovate/bps-bright-spots/intrepid-academy-at-hale

Irvin, E. (2018, October 7). A student's perspective on urban place-based ed [blog post]. Retrieved from *Getting Smart* at www.gettingsmart.com/2018/10/a-students -perspective-on-urban-place-based-ed

Jacobs, J. (1992). *The death and life of great American cities.* New York: Vintage Books.

Jeder, D. (2014). Transdisciplinary—The advantage of a holistic approach to life. *Procedia—Social and Behavioral Sciences, 137,* 127–131.

Josephs, M. (2018a). Real work—Olivia Ho [video file]. Retrieved from https://vimeo .com/292238281

Josephs, M. (2018b). Real work—Omari Anderson [video file]. Retrieved from https://vimeo.com/295472004

Keane, J. (2016, January 20). Let students lead: How local investigations drive democratic and global learning [blog post]. Retrieved from *Medium* at https://medium.com /global-perspectives/let-students-lead-how-local-investigations-drive-democratic -and-global-learning-e275454fe177

Knowles, G. (2019, January 16). Visible difference [tweet]. Retrieved from https://twitter.com/GrantLearns/status/1085566473832226817

Ladson-Billings, G. (1995). But that's just good teaching! The case for culturally relevant pedagogy, *Theory Into Practice, 34*(3), 159–165.

Lane-Zucker, L. (2016, August 01). Place-based education, entrepreneurship and invest- ing for an "impact economy" [blog post]. Retrieved from *Your Mark on the World* at https://yourmarkontheworld.com/place-based-education-entrepreneurship -investing-impact-economy

Lathram, B., & Frishman, A. (2016, September 4). 6 reasons you should work in America's parks and forests [blog post]. Retrieved from *Getting Smart* at www.gettingsmart .com/2016/09/work-and-learn-in-a-national-park

Lee, J. (2017, January 5). Unlocking the door to my future [blog post]. Retrieved from *Education Reimagined* at https://education-reimagined.org/unlocking-door -future

Liebtag, E. (2015). *International student teaching: A multi-case study about the inter- cultural competence of pre-service teachers.* University of Virginia. doi:10.18130 /V33R97

Liebtag, E. (2017a, April 25). An innovative K–8 human-centered approach at Design39 [blog post]. Retrieved from *Getting Smart* at www.gettingsmart.com/2017/04 /design39campus-innovative-k-8

Liebtag, E. (2017b, February 14). Houston high schools provide career options and choice for students [blog post]. Retrieved from *Getting Smart* at www.gettingsmart.com/2017/02/houston-high-schools-career-options-choice

Liebtag, E. (2017c, April 17). Rethinking middle school with design thinking at Vista Innovation & Design Academy [blog post]. Retrieved from *Getting Smart* at www.gettingsmart.com/2017/04/middle-school-design-thinking-vida

Liebtag, E. (2018, October 23). HQPBL case study: Energy Institute High School [blog post]. Retrieved from *Getting Smart* at www.gettingsmart.com/2018/10/hqpbl-case-study-energy-institute-high-school

Liebtag, E. (2019, January 2). Making the city the text at High Tech High [blog post]. Retrieved from *Getting Smart* at www.gettingsmart.com/2019/01/making-the-city-the-text-at-high-tech-high-pod-repost

Lindsay, J. (2017). Connecting beyond the classroom—Move from local to global learning modes. *Scan, 36*(2), 27–38.

Martin, K. (2018). *Learner centered innovation: Spark curiosity, ignite passion and unleash genius*. IMPress.

Mastery Transcript Consortium. (n.d.). Home page. Retrieved from https://mastery.org

McBride, J. (2016, August 9). Place-based professional learning in the New Tech Network [blog post]. Retrieved from *Getting Smart* at www.gettingsmart.com/2016/08/place-based-professional-learning-in-the-new-tech-network

Nadworny, E. (Writer). (2019, February 13). How high-crime neighborhoods make it harder for kids to show up at school [transcript, radio series episode]. *MindShift.* San Francisco: KQED.

National Equity Project. (n.d.). Why equity? Retrieved from http://nationalequityproject.org/about/equity

Nellie Mae Education Foundation. (2014). Putting students at the center: A reference guide. Retrieved from www.nmefoundation.org/getmedia/7fe89c01-dc9c-496f-80ed-1a53f25d593f/NMEF-sclreframeweb2

New Harmony High School. (n.d.). Our vision. Retrieved from https://newharmonyhigh.org/vision

Next Generation Science Standards. (n.d.). Science and engineering practices (SEP). Retrieved from www.nextgenscience.org/glossary/science-and-engineering-practices-sep

NGLC MyWays. (n.d.). What learners need to thrive in a world of change [blog post]. Retrieved from *NGLC MyWays* at https://myways.nextgenlearning.org

Normal Park Museum Magnet School (n.d.). Who we are. Retrieved from www.normalpark.com/apps/pages/index.jsp?uREC_ID=1087567&type=d&pREC_ID=1373523

Parsons, J., & Taylor, L. (2011). Improving student engagement. *Current Issues in Education, 14*(1). Retrieved from https://cie.asu.edu/ojs/index.php/cieatasu/article/view/745

Partridge, J. (2016, December 22). Higher ed approaches to empowering students [blog post]. Retrieved from *Getting Smart* at www.gettingsmart.com/2016/12/highered-approaches-empowering-students

PBL Works. (n.d.). What is project based learning? Retrieved from www.pblworks.org/what-is-pbl

Poth, R. D. (2018, November 8). Going global with virtual field trips [blog post]. Retrieved from *Getting Smart* at www.gettingsmart.com/2018/11/going-global-with-virtual-field-trips

Powell, A., Kennedy, K., & Patrick, S. (2013). Mean what you say: Defining and integrating personalized, blended and competency education [blog post]. Retrieved from *iNACOL* at www.inacol.org/resource/mean-what-you-say-defining-and-integrating-personalized-blended-and-competency-education

Pujar, N. (2016, May 29). Pod C kindergartners imagine their dream houses [blog post]. Retrieved from *D39C* at http://design39campus.com/connect/blog/2016/5/29/pod-c-kindergartners-imagine-their-dream-houses

Rabuzzi, D. (2016, November 21). Putting the city at the heart of place-based education [blog post]. Retrieved from *Getting Smart* at www.gettingsmart.com/2016/11/putting-the-city-at-the-heart-of-learning

Reidmiller, D. R., Avery, C. W., Easterling, D. R., Kunkel, K. E., Lewis, K. L. M., Maycock, T. K., et al. (Eds.). (2018). *Fourth national climate assessment. Vol. II: Impacts, risks, and adaptation in the United States*: Washington, DC: U.S. Global Change Research Program.

Remake Learning. (n.d.). About Remake Learning. Retrieved from https://remakelearning.org/about

Remake Learning. (n.d.). Home page. Retrieved from https://remakelearning.org

Scharmer, C. O. (2016). *Theory U: Leading from the future as it emerges* (2nd ed.). San Francisco: Berrett-Koehler.

Science Education Research Center at Carleton College. (n.d.) Why teach with an interdisciplinary approach? Retrieved from https://serc.carleton.edu/econ/interdisciplinary/why.html

Shapiro, T., Meschede, T., & Osoro, S. (2013). *The roots of the widening racial wealth gap: Explaining the black-white economic divide.* Waltham, MA: Brandeis Univeristy, Institute on Assets and Social Policy.

Share your learning. (n.d.). Retrieved from www.shareyourlearning.org

Skenazy, M. (2018, February). Jon Anderson with his student, Vidal Carrillo. Retrieved from www.honored.org/honoree/jon-anderson

Smith, G. (2016, November 3). The past, present and future of place-based learning [blog post]. Retrieved from *Getting Smart* at www.gettingsmart.com/2016/11/past-present-and-future-of-place-based-learning

Sobel, D. (2005). *Place-based education: Connecting classroom and community.* Great Barrington, MA: Orion Society.

Stanford d.school. (n.d.). Home page. Retrieved from https://dschool.stanford.edu

Stanford History Education Group. (2016). *Evaluating information: The cornerstone of civic online reasoning.* Retrieved from https://stacks.stanford.edu/file/druid:fv751yt5934/SHEG%20Evaluating%20Information%20Online.pdf

STAR School's Story. (2016, April 27). Retrieved from https://azcharters.org/star-schools-story

Stember, M. (1991). Advancing the social sciences through the interdisciplinary enterprise. *The Social Sciences Journal, 28*(1), 1–14.

Student Stories. (n.d.). Home page. Retrieved from https://mojopi.github.io/learning-lab/stories

Teton Science Schools. (n.d.). Place-based education. Retrieved from www.tetonscience
.org/about/place-based-education

Teton Science Schools. (2019, February 7). Place Network students making a big impact
with tiny home project [blog post]. Retrieved from *Teton Science Schools* at www.
tetonscience.org/place-network-students-making-a-big-impact-with-tiny-home
-project

Tinkergarten. (n.d.). About us. Retrieved from www.tinkergarten.com/about-us

Toshalis, E., & Nakkula, M. J. (2012). *Motivation, engagement, and student voice.*
Retrieved from www.nmefoundation.org/getmedia/e5cef30c-5935-434e-a360
-aea3e5d70dd2/Motivation-Engagement-Student-Voice-Students-at-the-Center

Vander Ark, T. (2016, November 4). Cool schools: 3 high school options in Tacoma
[blog post]. Retrieved from *Getting Smart* at www.gettingsmart.com/2016/11/cool
-schools-3-high-school-options-in-tacoma

Vander Ark, T. (2017, April 14). New Tech Network powers a common learning model &
unique missions [blog post]. Retrieved from *Getting Smart* at www.gettingsmart.com
/2017/04/new-tech-network-common-learning-model

Vander Ark, T. (2018a, May 2). Business partners define badges for San Diego students
[blog post]. *Education Week.* Retrieved from https://blogs.edweek.org/edweek/on
_innovation/2018/05/business_partners_define_badges_for_san_diego_students.html

Vander Ark, T. (2018b, April 24). Community defined projects at Health Leadership
High [blog post]. Retrieved from *Getting Smart* at www.gettingsmart.com/2018/04
/community-defined-projects-at-health-leadership-high

Vander Ark, T. (2018c, January 29). Design thinking and other learning priorities to
educate today's students for the coming automation economy [blog post]. Retrieved
from *Getting Smart* at www.gettingsmart.com/2018/01/design-thinking-other
-priorities-education-automation

Vander Ark, T. (2018d, November 27). The progressive schools of Philadelphia [blog
post]. Retrieved from *Getting Smart* at www.gettingsmart.com/2018/11/the
-progressive-schools-of-philadelphia

Vander Ark, T. (2018e, November 13). Santa Ana USD provides next-gen CTE pathways [blog post]. Retrieved from *Getting Smart* at www.gettingsmart.com/2018/11
/santa-ana-usd-provides-next-gen-cte-pathways

Vander Ark, T. (2018f, December 27). Top education trend of 2018: Active learning
spaces [blog post]. Retrieved from *Getting Smart* at www.gettingsmart.com/2018
/12/top-education-trend-of-2018-active-learning-spaces

Walker, T. D. (2016, September 15). Kindergarten, naturally. *The Atlantic.* Retrieved from
www.theatlantic.com/education/archive/2016/09/kindergarten-naturally/500138

Washor, E. (2018, December 2). Getting centered by going to the edge [blog post].
Retrieved from *Getting Smart* at www.gettingsmart.com/2018/12/getting-centered
-by-going-to-the-edge/?utm_campaign=coschedule&utm_source=twitter&utm
_medium=Getting_Smart&utm_content=Getting Centered by Going to the Edge

Whyte, D. (2016). The conversational nature of reality [podcast]. Retrieved from https://
onbeing.org/programs/david-whyte-the-conversational-nature-of-reality-dec2018

Wikipedia. (2019). Forest kindergarten. Retrieved from https://en.wikipedia.org/wiki
/Forest_kindergarten

William and Flora Hewlett Foundation. (2013, April). *Deeper learning competencies.* Retrieved from www.hewlett.org/wp-content/uploads/2016/08/Deeper_Learning _Defined_April_2013.pdf

Williams, C. (2018, April 26). The perks of a play-in-the-mud educational philosophy. *The Atlantic.* Retrieved from www.theatlantic.com/education/archive/2018/04 /early-childhood-outdoor-education/558959

XQ. (2017, Fall). Grand Rapids Public Museum School. Retrieved from https://assets.ctfas sets.net/35eubtuv0bcm/2seF7MiZSYEiSKIGcWWgO0/a3e3a90454d9dc754baae 617581fc57f/GRPMS.pdf

XQ. (n.d. a). This is Círculos. Retrieved from https://xqsuperschool.org/xq-schools/circulos

XQ. (n.d. b). This is Iowa BIG. Retrieved from https://xqsuperschool.org/xq-schools /iowa-big

Your Place Matters. (2018). On *We're Doing It Wrong* podcast. Retrieved from https://podcasts.apple.com/us/podcast/were-doing-it-wrong/id1365700082

Index

The letter f following a page number denotes a figure. The letter *g* denotes a term found in the glossary.

ACE Leadership High School, 47–48
agency, 5*f*, 10, 87–89
Albemarle County Public Schools, 72–73
Anthropocene, 132
arts, implementation setting for, 101
attention, focused, 7*f*
augmented reality (AR), 18–19
augmented screens and spaces, mixed reality, 18–19
authentic learning, 55–56
Authentic partners and audiences (take action), 96, 127

belonging, 7*f*, 26–27
big-data analysis, 55
Big data and data analysis sprints (take action), 60–61, 123
blended learning, 134*g*

bonding, 12
Build your first project (take action), 96, 126–127

Círculos, 33–34
Classroom
    rethink the (take action), 83, 125–126
    take students out of the (take action), 34, 35, 120
Classroom openers (take action), 62, 123
cognition, 7*f*, 8*f*
cognitive load, manageable, 7*f*
colleges and universities, implementation at, 102
community, 5*f*, 90–91
community as classroom
    building belonging, 26–27
    competency-based, 42–44
    design principle, 3*f*

implementation action steps, 34–37
implementation methods and
    approaches, 29
inquiry and, 55–56
inquiry-based learning in, 52–53
introduction, 21–22
learning sciences connection, 37
museum partnership example, 24–26
principles, 22–24, 104
relationships and connections,
    exploring, 24–26
sample agreement, 35*f*
social capital, investing in, 27–28
stakeholder starting points, 119–121
technologies role in, 28
community as classroom, cases
  illustrating
    Círculos, 33–34
    Hana high and elementary school,
        30–31
    Hartford Heritage Project, Capital
        Community College, 32
community as classroom, take action
  points for teachers and stakeholders
    build a community map, 34, 119
    consider joint facilities, 36–37, 121
    create community partnership
        programs, 34, 120
    do a community deep dive, 36, 120
    explore your own place with family
        and friends, 34, 119
    survey your parent body for
        "challenges" worth addressing,
        34–35, 120
    take advantage of internships, 36, 121
    take students out of the classroom, 34,
        35, 120
    visit local historical sites, 36, 120
    write a digital community newspaper,
        35–36, 120
community-building, 12
Community deep dive (take action), 36,
  120
Community map, build a (take action),
  34, 119

Community opportunity surveys (take
    action), 83, 125
Community Partner Program Agreement,
    116*f*
Community partnership programs (take
    action), 34, 120
community spaces, implementation at, 103
competency-based education, 42–44, 134*g*
confirmation inquiry, 53–54
contexts for learning, 13–16
control, sense of, 7*f*
Cottonwood School for Civics and
    Science, 57–58
cultural context for learning, 13*f*, 15–16

Daily goals and reflection as habits (take
    action), 49, 122
Decision making, design thinking process
    in (take action), 83, 126
deeper learning, 134*g*
Del Lago Academy, 46–47
Design39Campus, 82
Design challenges (take action), 83, 126
design thinking
    defined, 134*g*
    design principle, 3*f*
    learning sciences connection, 84
    principles, 75–76, 78, 104
    stakeholder starting points, 125–126
    take action steps, 83
design thinking, cases illustrating
    Design39Campus, 82
    Grand Rapids Public Museum School,
        74–75
    Normal Park Museum School, 80–81
    University Charter School, 82
design thinking, take action points for
  teachers and stakeholders
    conduct community opportunity
        surveys, 83, 125
    connect with industry to create,
        83–84, 126
    create mini makerspaces, 83, 126
    embed the design-thinking process in
        decision making, 83, 126

design thinking, take action points for
  teachers and stakeholders, (cont'd)
    have students generate challenges
      worth solving, 83, 126
    present design challenges, 83, 126
    rethink the classroom, 83, 125–126
    support a student-run business, 83,
      126
design thinking process
  constraints, 78
  evaluating for innovation, 79f
  Stanford d.school, 76
  Teton Science Schools, 76, 77f, 78
Design-thinking process in decision
  making, embedding (take action), 83,
  126
developmental state, 7f
difference, making a, 132–133
Digital community newspapers (take
  action), 35–36, 72, 120, 124

Eagle Rock School, 91–93
education
  competency-based, 134g
  early, implementation setting, 102
  industrial model of, 1–2
  place-based, 134g
emotions, constructive, 7f
empathy, 66
encoding, meaningful, 7f
Energy Institute High School, 95
engagement, 44
environmental context for learning,
  13f, 15
equity
  building through multiple
    perspectives, 89–90
  community as classroom and, 27–28
  defined, 5f
  local to global, 65–66
  promoting place, 11
Exports and imports, study (take action),
  73, 125

feedback, high-quality, 7f
future, the, 132–133

Genius hour (take action), 49, 122
Global connections to gain intercultural
  understandings (take action), 73, 125
Global opportunities, connect for (take
  action), 72, 125
Goals and reflection as habits (take
  action), 49, 122
Grand Rapids Public Museum School,
  74–75
guided inquiry, 54

Hana high and elementary school, 30–31
Hartford Heritage Project, Capital
  Community College, 32
High Tech High, 58–59
Historical sites, visit local (take action),
  36, 120
hyper individualism, 131

identity, 7f, 8f
immersive screens, mixed reality, 19
implementation activities
  build, revise, and implement, 113, 114f
  build a community partner program,
    115, 116f
  build student ownership and skills,
    114, 114f, 115f
  conduct action research, 117, 118f
  do place-based research, 107, 111, 112f
  explore the place triangle, 114, 115f
  find peer or community partners, 115,
    116f, 117f
  identify challenges and opportunities,
    107
  inquire into place, 106f, 107, 107f,
    108–110f, 111f
  map your place, 107, 111f
  measure outcomes, share successes,
    115–116, 117, 119f
  self-assessment and observation tool,
    107, 108–110f
  start small, 113, 114f
implementation assistance
  parents or guardians, 129
  policy makers, 128–129
  schools, 130
  students, 129–130

implementation process
    barriers to, 117, 119
    introduction, 98–99
    six phases of, 106*f*
industrial model of education, 1–2
Industry, connect with (take action),
    83–84, 126
inquiry-based learning
    authentic learning and, 55–56
    design principle, 3*f*
    learning sciences connection, 62
    levels of, 53–55
    preference for, 56–57
    principles, 52–53, 104
    student thoughts on, 52
inquiry-based learning, cases illustrating
    Cottonwood School for Civics and
      Science, 57–58
    High Tech High, 58–59
    Science and Math Institute, 59–60
    take action steps, 60–62
inquiry-based learning, take action points
  for teachers and stakeholders
    ask students to share questions about
      their community, 124
    assign mini research projects, 62, 123
    engage students in phenology, 62,
      123–124
    incorporate big data and data analysis
      sprints, 60–61, 123
    participate in interdisciplinary
      educator experiences, 124
    set up question walls, 62, 123
    take a walk, 62, 123
    use classroom openers, 62, 123
    use survey tools, 62, 123
instructional context for learning, 13*f*, 14
interdisciplinary
    building agency through Project Based
      Learning, 87–89
    building community in an
      interdisciplinary world, 90–91
    building equity through multiple
      perspectives, 89–90
    design principle, 3*f*
    learning sciences connection, 97

    principles, 86–87, 104
    stakeholder starting points, 126–128
    student thoughts on, 85–86
    take action steps, 96–97
interdisciplinary, cases illustrating
    Eagle Rock School, 91–93
    Energy Institute High School, 95
    Lake Elementary School, 93–94
interdisciplinary, take action points for
  teachers and stakeholders
    build your first project, 96, 126–127
    develop interdisciplinary driving
      questions, 96, 127
    explore place-based postsecondary
      programs, 96, 127
    meld place-based learning into
      coplanning across disciplines, 96, 127
    seek authentic partners and
      audiences, 96, 127
    visit another classroom, 96, 127
Interdisciplinary driving questions (take
  action), 96, 127
Interdisciplinary educator experiences,
  participate in (take action), 124
international setting for implementation,
  103–104
Internships, take advantage of (take
  action), 36, 121
Iowa BIG, 38–40

Joint facilities, consider (take action),
  36–37, 121

Kern Entrepreneurship Education
  Network (KEEN), 132

Lake Elementary School, 93–94
Leadership opportunities (take action),
  49, 121
learner-centered education
    competency-based system, 42–44
    design principle, 3*f*
    five elements of, 41*f*
    from delivering content to
      co-constructing and facilitating
      learning, 44–45

learner-centered education, (*cont'd*)
    implementation action steps, 48–50
    the learner in, 41
    learning sciences connection, 48–50
    on personalization, 45
    place, importance of, 44
    principles, 40–44, 104
    student example, 38–40
learner-centered education, cases
  illustrating
    ACE Leadership High School, 47–48
    Del Lago Academy, 46–47
learner-centered education, take action
  points for teachers and stakeholders
    conduct student-led conferences, 49,
      121–122
    create a "genius" hour, 49, 122
    encourage leadership opportunities,
      49, 121
    make daily goals and reflection a habit,
      49, 122
    move toward self-directed learning,
      49–50, 122
    use competency-based report cards,
      49, 122
learning
    deeper, 134*g*
    industrialization of, 1–2
    personalized, 134*g*
    project-based, 135*g*
    student-centered, 135*g*
Learning community, build a (take
  action), 125
learning differences, 7*f*
learning sciences
    defined, 6
    principles, 7*f*, 8*f*. *see also specific*
      principles
life experiences, 7*f*
local to global
    benefits of, 65
    design principle, 3*f*
    introduction, 63–64
    learning sciences connection, 73
    in practice, 66–67

    principles, 104
    stakeholder starting points, 124–125
    student example, 64, 65–66
    technology and, 67–68
local to global, cases illustrating
    Albemarle County Public Schools,
      72–73
    Oso New Tech High School, 68–69
    Teton Science Schools, 70
local to global, take action points for
  teachers and stakeholders
    build a learning community, 125
    build a local to global news wall, 72,
      124
    connect globally to gain intercultural
      understandings, 73, 125
    connect to a global opportunity, 72,
      125
    connect virtually with another school,
      73, 125
    create a digital community newspaper,
      72, 124
    create a virtual reality experience, 72,
      124
    study exports and imports, 73, 125
    try a project with a global-issue focus
      and make local connections, 73, 125

Metropolitan Regional Career and
  Technical Center (MET), 63–64
Mini makerspaces (take action), 83, 126
Mini research projects (take action), 62,
  123
mixed reality, 18–20
motivation, 7*f*, 8*f*, 43
motivational context for learning, 13–14,
  13*f*
museum partnerships, 24–26
museums, 101

National Equity Project, 5*f*
Newspapers, digital community (take
  action), 35–36, 72, 120, 124
News walls (take action), 72, 124
Normal Park Museum School, 80–81

open inquiry, 54
original inquiry, 56
Oso New Tech High School, 68–69

parents, stakeholder starting points for
    get connected, 129
    listen to your child's stories about
        place, 129
    share your experience, 129
    talk with teachers, 129
    tell your story, 129
Parents, survey for challenges worth
    addressing (take action), 34–35, 120
parks, implementation at, 101–102
Partners and audiences, seek authentic
    (take action), 96, 127
personalized learning, 12, 17, 45, 134g
Phenology, engage students in (take
    action), 62, 123–124
place
    components of, 22, 23f
    as an ethic, 131–132
    as pedagogy, 131–132
place, contexts for learning
    cultural, 13f, 15–16
    environmental, 13f, 15
    instructional, 13f, 14
    motivational, 13–14, 13f
place, elements promoted by
    agency, 10
    community-building, 12
    equity, 11
Place, exploring with family and friends
    (take action), 34, 119
place-based education (PBE). See also
    specific principles
    defined, 134g
    design principle, 3f
    ethic of contribution, 2–3
    future of, 132–133
    how-to guide, 98–99
    importance of place in, 9–10, 23
    learning science principles alignment,
        6, 7f, 8f
    place-based resources, 105

principles review, 104
    settings for, 99–104
    student example, 38–40
    student thoughts on, 9, 21–22
place-based education (PBE), factors
    driving
    accessible transportation to extend
        access, 20
    competency education, 18
    components, 16f
    mixed reality, 18–20
    mixed reality technologies, 18–20
    personalized learning, 17
place-based learning, context and, 9–10,
    13–16, 13f
Place-based learning into coplanning
    across disciplines (take action), 96, 127
Place-based postsecondary programs
    (take action), 96, 127
place mindset, 132
Place Triangle, 22, 23f
policy makers, stakeholder starting
    points for
    consider weighted funding, 128
    do a policy refresh, 128
    review transportation budgets, 128
    revise master schedules, 128
    seek financial support, 128
    tap into community assets, 128–129
practice, effective, 7f
project-based learning, 14, 135g
Projects with a global-issue focus and make
    local connections (take action), 73, 125

questions
    Interdisciplinary driving questions
        (take action), 96, 127
    Students share questions about their
        community (take action), 124
Question walls (take action), 62, 123

relationships and connections, exploring,
    24
Report cards, use competency-based
    (take action), 49, 122

Research projects, mini (take action), 62, 123

rippers and weavers, 131

rural setting for implementation, 100

schools, stakeholder starting points for
    advocate for your interests, 129–130
    build an "innovation" mindset in your school, 130
    commit to long-term implementation, 130
    complete an asset map, 130
    find funding sources, 130
    find networks and models, 130
    measure and celebrate results, 130
    reach out to partner schools, 130
Science and Math Institute, 59–60
Science Leadership Academy (SLA), 51–52
screens, mixed reality, 18
Self-directed learning (take action), 49–50, 122
self-efficacy, 7f
self-understanding, 7f
social capital, 12, 27–28
stakeholder starting points. See also teachers and stakeholders entries
    stakeholder starting points. see also teachers and stakeholders entries
stakeholder starting points for parents
    get connected, 129
    listen to your child's stories about place, 129
    share your experience, 129
    talk with teachers, 129
    tell your story, 129
stakeholder starting points for policy makers
    consider weighted funding, 128
    do a policy refresh, 128
    review transportation budgets, 128
    revise master schedules, 128
    seek financial support, 128
    tap into community assets, 128–129
stakeholder starting points for schools
    advocate for your interests, 129–130
    build an "innovation" mindset in your school, 130

commit to long-term implementation, 130
    complete an asset map, 130
    find funding sources, 130
    find networks and models, 130
    measure and celebrate results, 130
    reach out to partner schools, 130
stakeholder starting points for students
    advocate for your interests, 129–130
    complete an asset map, 130
    get outside, 129
    tell your story, 129
    unpack equity, 129
Stanford d.school, 76
State Education and Environment Roundtable (SEER), 15
structured inquiry, 54
student-centered learning, 135g
Student-led conferences (take action), 49, 121–122
Student-run business (take action), 83, 126
students, stakeholder starting points for
    advocate for your interests, 129–130
    complete an asset map, 130
    get outside, 129
    tell your story, 129
    unpack equity, 129
Students generate challenges worth solving (take action), 83, 126
Students share questions about their community (take action), 124
Study exports and imports (take action), 73, 125
Survey tools (take action), 62, 123

Take students out of the classroom (take action), 34, 35, 120
teachers and stakeholders take action points for community as classroom
    build a community map, 34, 119
    consider joint facilities, 36–37, 121
    create community partnership programs, 34, 120
    do a community deep dive, 36, 120
    explore your own place with family and friends, 34, 119

survey your parent body for "challenges" worth addressing, 34–35, 120

take advantage of internships, 36, 121

take students out of the classroom, 34, 35, 120

take your students out of the classroom, 35

visit local historical sites, 36, 120

write a digital community newspaper, 35–36, 120

teachers and stakeholders take action points for design thinking

conduct community opportunity surveys, 83, 125

connect with industry to create, 83–84, 126

create mini makerspaces, 83, 126

embed the design-thinking process in decision making, 83, 126

have students generate challenges worth solving, 83, 126

present design challenges, 83, 126

rethink the classroom, 83, 125–126

support a student-run business, 83, 126

teachers and stakeholders take action points for inquiry-based learning

ask students to share questions about their community, 124

assign mini research projects, 62, 123

engage students in phenology, 62, 123–124

incorporate big data and data analysis sprints, 60–61, 123

participate in interdisciplinary educator experiences, 124

set up question walls, 62, 123

take a walk, 62, 123

use classroom openers, 62, 123

use survey tools, 62, 123

teachers and stakeholders take action points for interdisciplinary

build your first project, 96, 126–127

develop interdisciplinary driving questions, 96, 127

explore place-based postsecondary programs, 96, 127

meld place-based learning into coplanning across disciplines, 96, 127

seek authentic partners and audiences, 96, 127

visit another classroom, 96, 127

teachers and stakeholders take action points for learner-centered education

conduct student-led conferences, 49, 121–122

create a "genius" hour, 49, 122

encourage leadership opportunities, 49, 121

make daily goals and reflection a habit, 49, 122

move toward self-directed learning, 49–50, 122

use competency-based report cards, 49, 122

teachers and stakeholders take action points for local to global

build a learning community, 125

build a local to global news wall, 72, 124

connect globally to gain intercultural understandings, 73, 125

connect to a global opportunity, 72, 125

connect virtually with another school, 73, 125

create a digital community newspaper, 72, 124

create a virtual reality experience, 72, 124

study exports and imports, 73, 125

try a project with a global-issue focus and make local connections, 73, 125

technology

local to global and, 67–68

role in community as classroom, 18–20, 28

Teton Science Schools, 70, 76, 77f, 78

Teton Science Schools Rubric, 108–110f

thinking, metacognitive, 7f

transportation access, challenge of, 20

travel-based learning, 15–16

universities, implementation at, 102
University Charter School, 82
urban setting for implementation, 99–100
Use classroom openers (take action), 123

value, 7f
variability, individual, 7f, 8f
Virtual connections with other schools (take action), 73, 125
virtual experiences, 103

virtual reality (VR), 19
Virtual reality experiences (take action), 72, 124
Visit another classroom (take action), 96, 127

Walks (take action), 62, 123
wayfinding abilities, 16
weavers and rippers, 131
Write a digital community newspaper (take action), 35–36, 120

About the Authors

Tom Vander Ark is an advocate for innovations in learning and the power of place. As CEO of Getting Smart, he advises school districts and networks, education foundations and funders, and impact organizations on the path forward. A prolific writer and speaker, Tom is the author of *Getting Smart, Smart Cities That Work for Everyone, Smart Parents,* and *Better Together* and has published thousands of articles as well as coauthoring more than 50 books and white papers. He writes regularly on GettingSmart.com and LinkedIn and contributes to *Forbes.*

Previously, Tom served as the first Executive Director of Education for the Bill & Melinda Gates Foundation and as a public school superintendent in Washington state. He has extensive private-sector experience and cofounded the first education venture fund, Learn Capital. Readers can connect with him on Twitter: @TvanderArk.

Emily Liebtag helps educators and communities dream of what's possible and then helps them do what it takes to achieve it. In her role as director, she leads Getting Smart's advocacy efforts, collaborating with educational organizations to create scalable strategies, thought leadership campaigns, industry research, and professional learning experiences.

Emily's experience as a teacher in a Title I elementary school in Durham, North Carolina, has informed her interest in place-based education and connections to community. She has also worked in higher education as a curriculum developer and researcher. Throughout her career, she has leveraged others' ideas to develop transformative learning experiences. She strongly believes that active approaches such as project-based learning are most successful when considered in the context of diversity and equity issues.

Emily holds a Doctor of Education degree in curriculum, teaching, and learning, with a focus on diversity and culture in education; a Master of Education degree in curriculum and instruction, with a focus on science education; and a Bachelor of Arts degree in elementary education. Readers can connect with her on Twitter: @EmilyLiebtag.

Nate McClennen is the leader of Teton Science Schools' Place Network Schools, a comprehensive K–12 blended-learning program that combines an online learning experience with a place-based approach to help students better understand and engage in local rural communities. He was part of the founding faculty at Teton Science Schools' Journeys School in 2001 and was appointed Head of School in 2006. Nate has been part of the leadership team at Teton Science Schools since 2011. In 2015, he became the Director of Education and Innovation, focusing on how to scale the impact of Teton Science Schools through technology, innovation, design learning, and school networks.

Nate has written and spoken extensively about place-based education. He is an active participant in Transcend Education's Yellow Hats League and

Education Reimagined's ILX Core Team—exploring the front end of learning. Over the course of his career, he has taught science and math at the secondary level and science at the university level. He believes that schools must connect students to communities in meaningful ways in order to increase the capacity of the next generation. Readers can connect with him on Twitter: @nmcclenn.

Related ASCD Resources: Place-Based Education

At the time of publication, the following resources were available (ASCD stock numbers in parentheses). For up-to-date information about ASCD resources, go to www.ascd.org. You can search the complete archives of *Educational Leadership* at www.ascd.org/el.

Print Products

Becoming a Globally Competent Teacher by Ariel Tichnor-Wagner, Hillary Parkhouse, Jocelyn Glazier, and J. Montana Cain (#119012)

Breaking Free from Myths About Teaching and Learning: Innovation as an Engine for Student Success by Allison Zmuda (#109041)

Cultivating Curiosity in K–12 Classrooms: How to Promote and Sustain Deep Learning by Wendy L. Ostroff (#116001)

Partnering with Parents to Ask the Right Questions: A Powerful Strategy for Strengthening School-Family Partnerships by Luz Santana, Dan Rothstein, and Agnes Bain (#117011)

Real-World Projects: How do I design relevant and engaging learning experiences? (ASCD Arias) (#SF115043)

ASCD myTeachSource®

Download resources from a professional learning platform with hundreds of research-based best practices and tools for your classroom at http://myteachsource.ascd.org/.

For more information, send an e-mail to member@ascd.org; call 1-800-933-2723 or 703-578-9600; send a fax to 703-575-5400; or write to Information Services, ASCD, 1703 N. Beauregard St., Alexandria, VA 22311-1714 USA.

WHOLE CHILD
TENETS

1 HEALTHY
Each student enters school healthy and learns about and practices a healthy lifestyle.

2 SAFE
Each student learns in an environment that is physically and emotionally safe for students and adults.

3 ENGAGED
Each student is actively engaged in learning and is connected to the school and broader community.

4 SUPPORTED
Each student has access to personalized learning and is supported by qualified, caring adults.

5 CHALLENGED
Each student is challenged academically and prepared for success in college or further study and for employment and participation in a global environment.

THE WHOLE CHILD

The ASCD Whole Child approach is an effort to transition from a focus on narrowly defined academic achievement to one that promotes the long-term development and success of all children. Through this approach, ASCD supports educators, families, community members, and policymakers as they move from a vision about educating the whole child to sustainable, collaborative actions.

The Power of Place relates to the **engaged, supported,** and **challenged** tenets.
For more about the ASCD Whole Child approach, visit
www.ascd.org/wholechild.